dabble lab

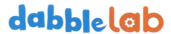

Manga Drawing with

DC

HOW TO DRAW BATMAN™ MANGA!

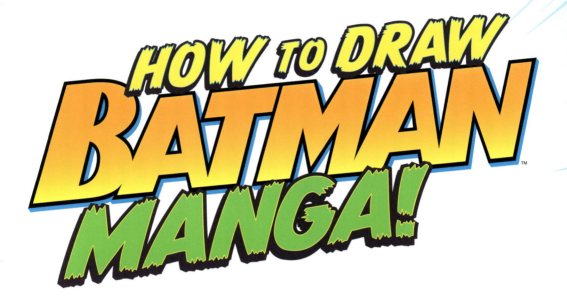

by Christopher Harbo

illustrated by Haining

Batman created by Bob Kane with Bill Finger

CAPSTONE PRESS
a capstone imprint

Published by Capstone Press, an imprint of Capstone.
1710 Roe Crest Drive
North Mankato, Minnesota 56003
capstonepub.com

Copyright © 2023 DC.
BATMAN and all related characters and elements © & ™ DC. (s23)

All rights reserved. No part of this publication may be reproduced in whole or in part, or stored in a retrieval system, or transmitted in any form or by any means, electronic, mechanical, photocopying, recording, or otherwise, without written permission of the publisher.

Library of Congress Cataloging-in-Publication Data
is available on the Library of Congress website.
ISBN: 9781669021582 (hardcover)
ISBN: 9781669021544 (ebook PDF)

Summary: Batman and manga unite! Put a new spin on classic Gotham City Super Heroes and Super-Villains, and learn how to draw them as dynamic manga characters with easy-to-follow steps.

Editorial Credits
Editor: Abby Huff; Designer: Hilary Wacholz;
Media Researcher: Jo Miller; Production Specialist: Tori Abraham

Image Credits
Photos: Capstone Studio: Karon Dubke 5 (all), Backgrounds and design elements: Capstone

The publisher and the author shall not be liable for any damages allegedly arising from the information in this book, and they specifically disclaim any liability from the use or application of any of the contents of this book.

TABLE OF CONTENTS

LEAP INTO MANGA! 4

THE MANGAKA'S TOOLKIT 5

BATMAN 6

ROBIN 8

BATGIRL 10

BATWING 12

BATWOMAN 14

CATWOMAN 16

THE JOKER 18

HARLEY QUINN 20

THE RIDDLER 22

POISON IVY 24

THE PENGUIN 26

BATMAN VS. CLAYFACE 28

MORE MANGA DRAWING FUN! 32

MORE DC SUPER HERO FUN! 32

LEAP INTO MANGA!

Batman has battled to keep the mean streets of Gotham City clean of crime for more than 80 years. In that time, his daring feats have come to life in comic books, TV shows, and mega-hit movies. But did you know the Dark Knight once made a giant leap across the Pacific Ocean? It's true! In 1966, *Batman* by Jiro Kuwata featured the Caped Crusader like he'd never been seen before—in Japanese manga!

What is manga? Simply put, it's comics and graphic novels from Japan. While the manga art style dates back more than 800 years, its popularity in books and magazines really exploded in the late 1940s. Since then, manga has become famous for its awesome art. Manga characters have large eyes, small noses and mouths, and pointed chins. And when it comes to heart-pounding action and dynamic scenes, few comics match manga's electric look. It's no wonder manga mania has spread all over the world!

SO DON'T WAIT ANOTHER SECOND! TAKE YOUR OWN GIANT LEAP BY REUNITING BATMAN WITH THE MANGA WORLD. DRAW YOUR FAVORITE GOTHAM CITY HEROES AND VILLAINS IN MANGA STYLE!

THE MANGAKA'S TOOLKIT

All manga artists—or mangaka—need the right tools to make amazing art. Gather the following supplies before you begin drawing:

PAPER

Art supply and hobby stores have many types of special drawing paper. But any blank, unlined paper will work well too.

PENCILS

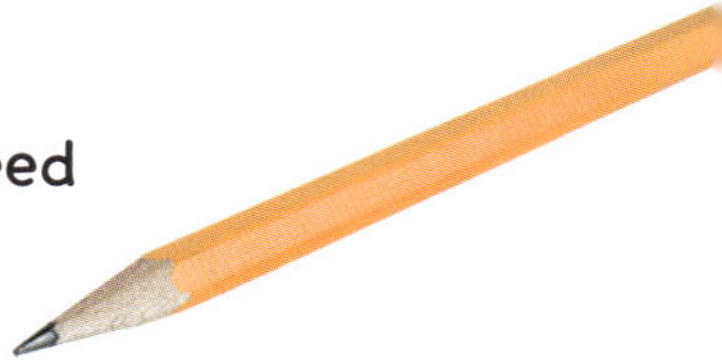

Sketch in pencil first. That way, if you make a mistake or need to change a detail, it's easy to erase and redraw.

PENCIL SHARPENER

Keep a good pencil sharpener within reach. Sharp pencils will help you draw clean lines.

ERASERS

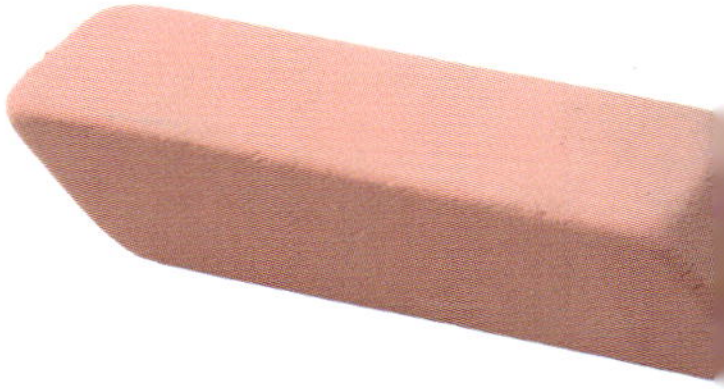

Making mistakes is a normal part of drawing. Regular pencil erasers work in a pinch. But high-quality rubber or kneaded erasers last longer and won't damage your paper.

BLACK MARKER PENS

When your sketch is done, trace over the final lines with a black marker pen. By "inking" the lines, your characters will practically leap off the page!

COLORED PENCILS AND MARKERS

While manga stories are usually created in black and white, they often have full-color covers. Feel free to complete your manga masterpiece with colored pencils and markers. There's nothing like a pop of color to bring characters to life!

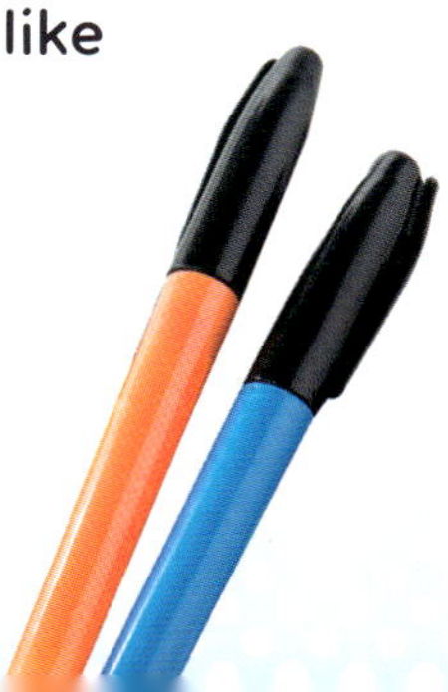

BATMAN

When the Bat-Signal blazes over Gotham City, the Dark Knight always answers the call. Leaping into action, he follows the clues to track down the world's worst Super-Villains. And when he finds his foes, the Caped Crusader grabs a Batarang from his Utility Belt, then lets it fly with a flick of the wrist!

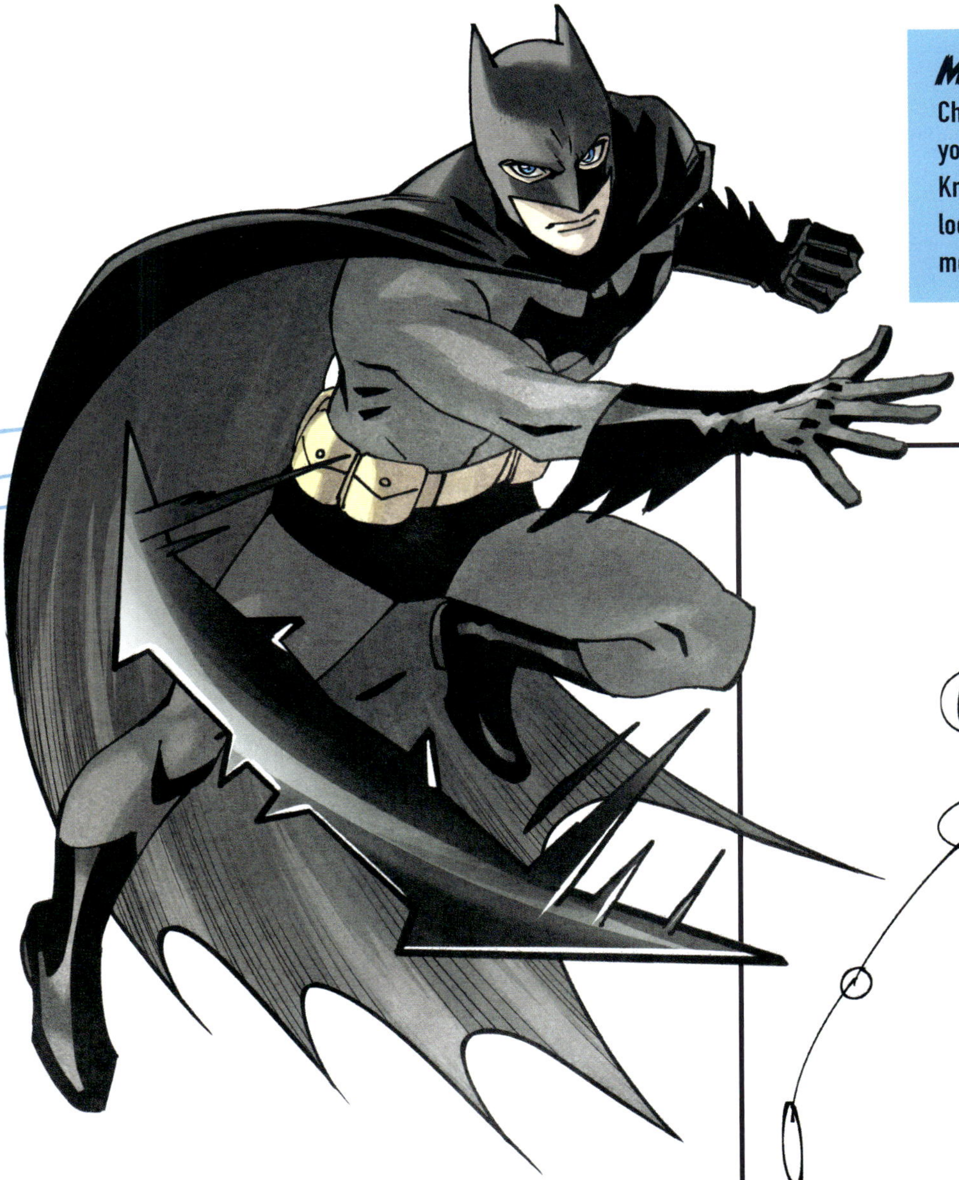

MANGA FACT

Check out library books that teach you how to draw the human form. Knowing how our bones and muscles look and move can help you create more lifelike characters.

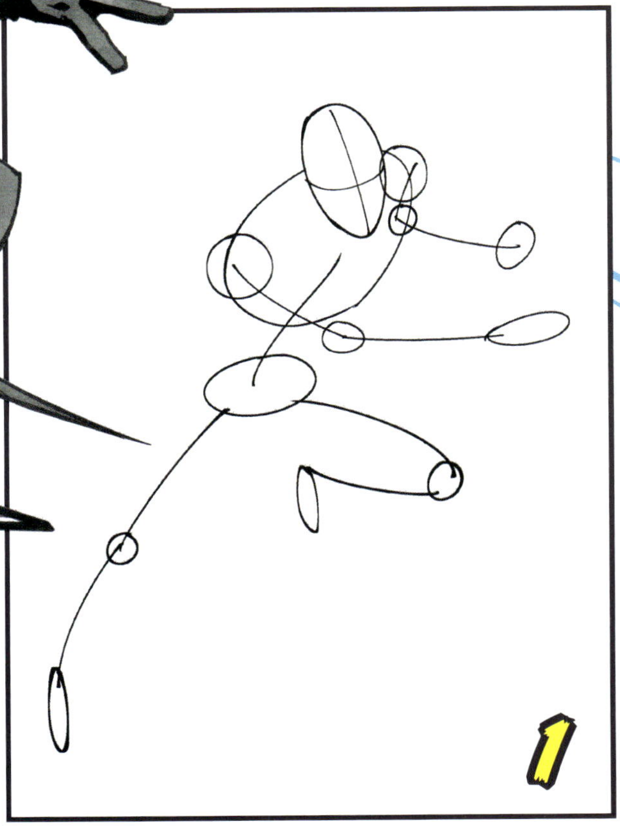
1

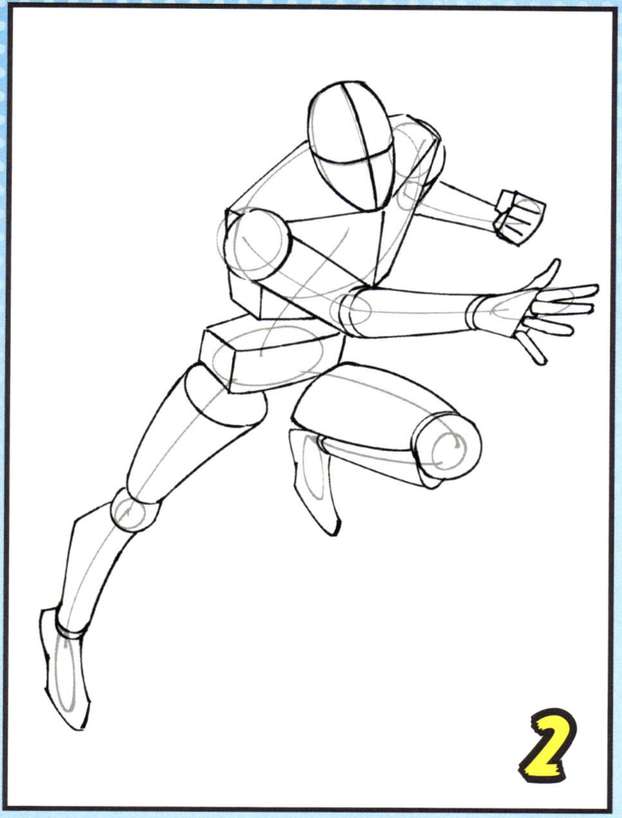
2

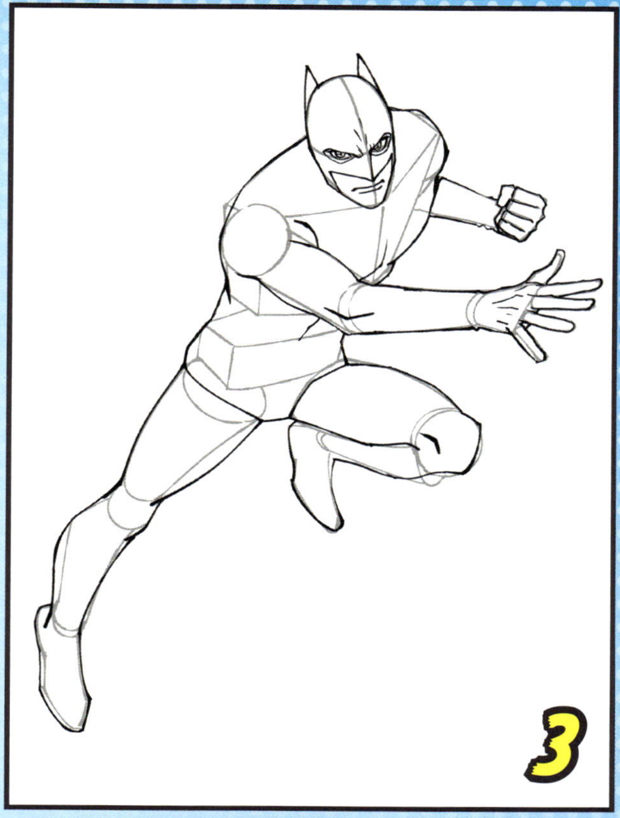
3

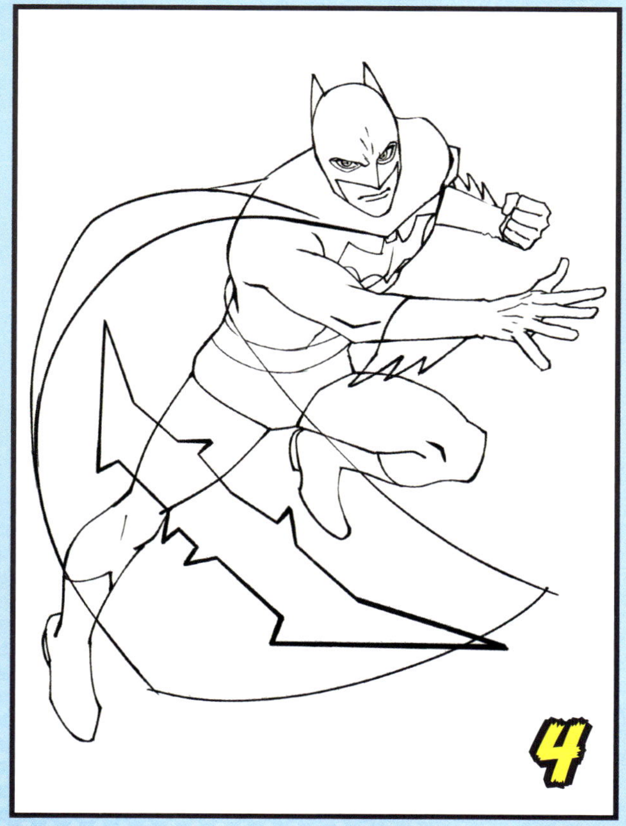
4

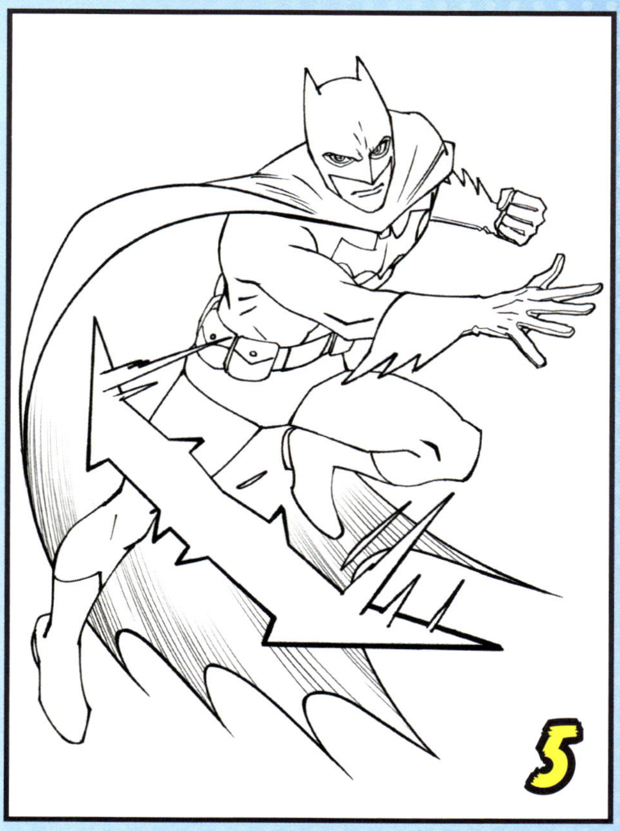
5

ROBIN

Few Super Hero sidekicks compare to Robin. His lightning-fast reflexes and quick wit are more than a match for any of Batman's baddies. Best of all, Robin is loyal and true. Whenever the Caped Crusader gets in a bind, he can count on the Boy Wonder to swoop down on a Batrope in the nick of time!

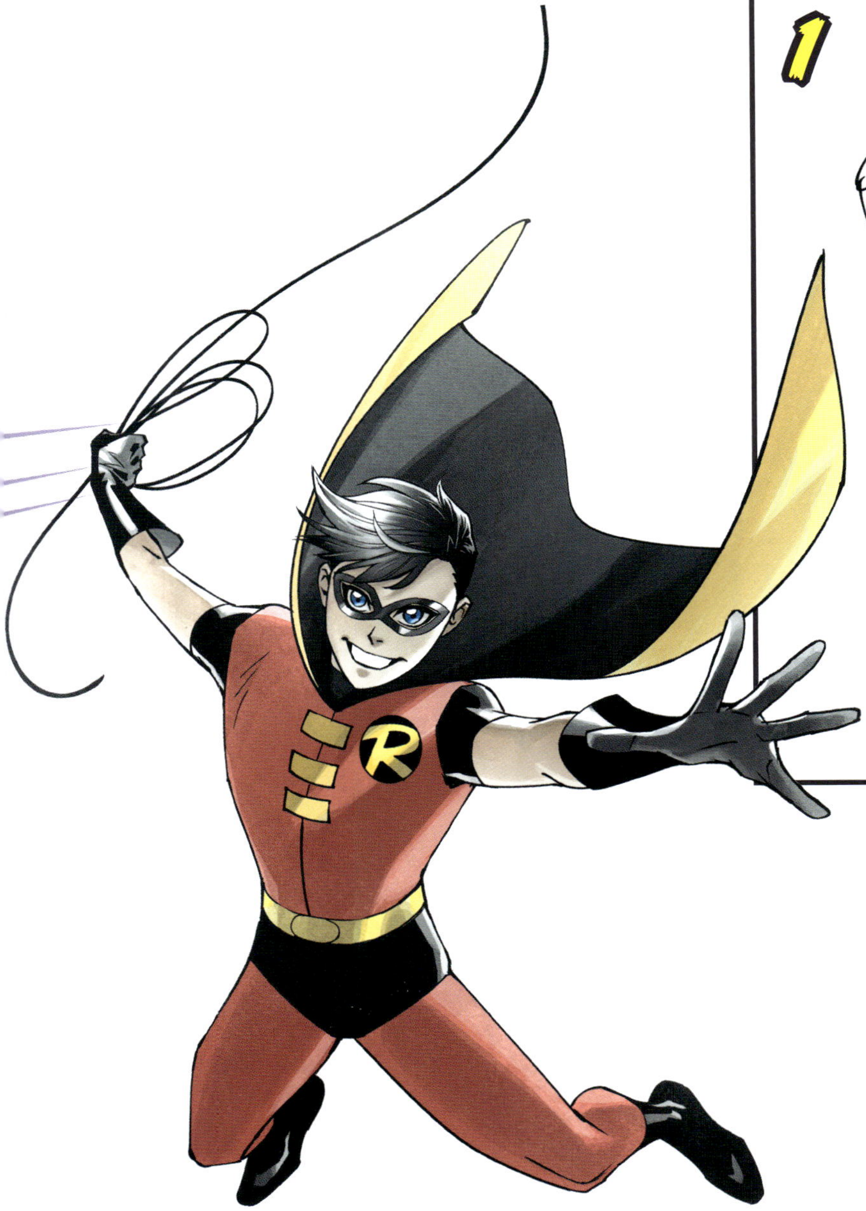

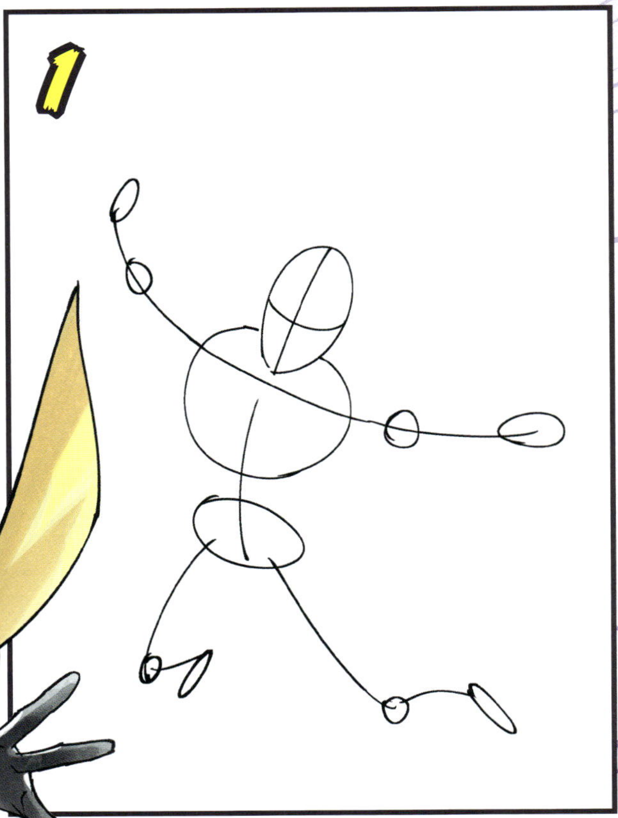
1

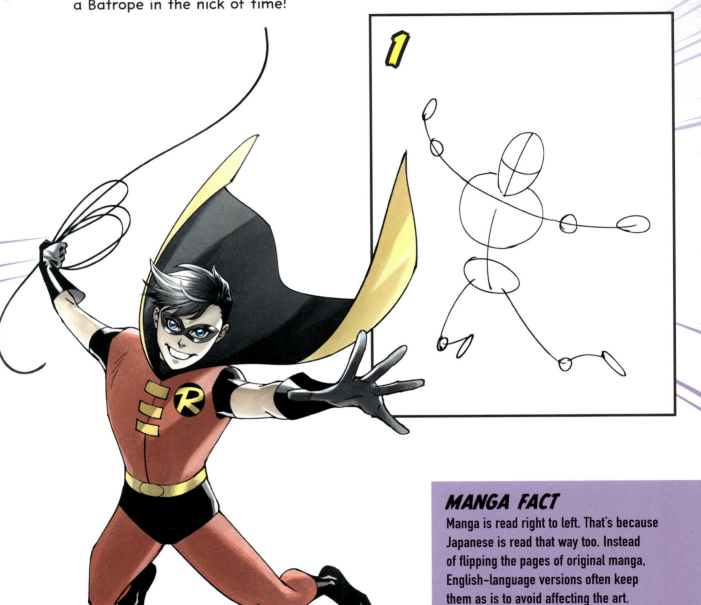

MANGA FACT

Manga is read right to left. That's because Japanese is read that way too. Instead of flipping the pages of original manga, English-language versions often keep them as is to avoid affecting the art.

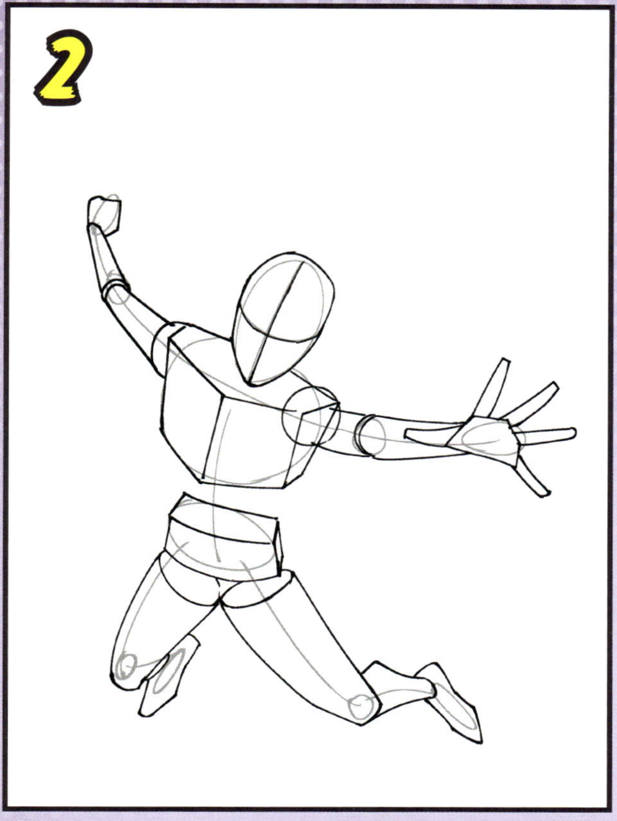
2

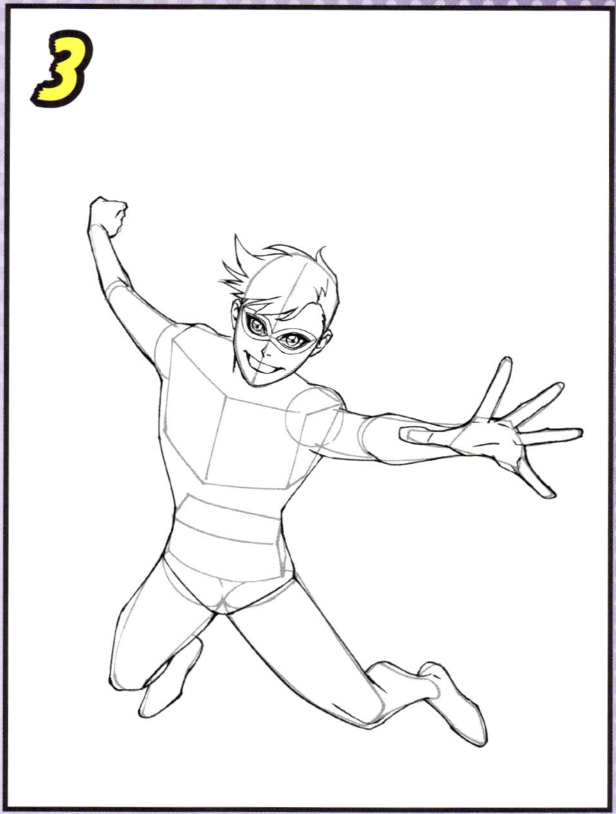
3

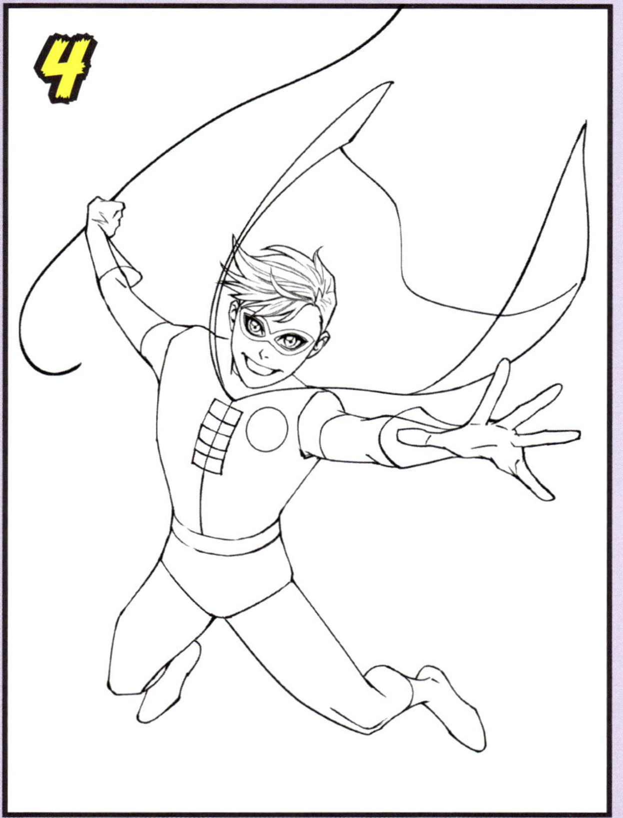
4

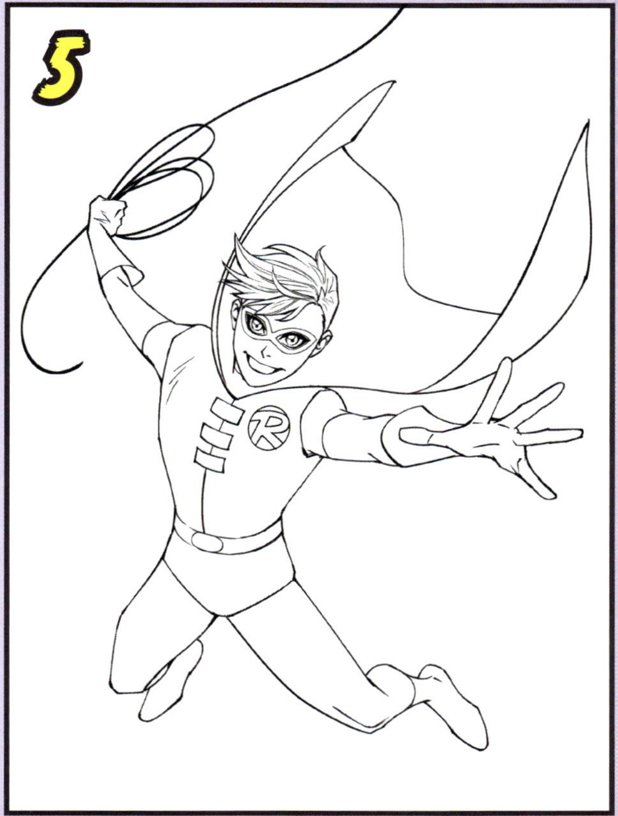
5

BATGIRL

Batgirl isn't about to let the Dynamic Duo have all the fun. Each night, this tech-savvy teen patrols Gotham City for coldhearted criminals. Will tonight be the night she hunts down Harley Quinn or rounds up the Riddler? Either way, this martial arts master is bound to have a blast kicking crime to the curb!

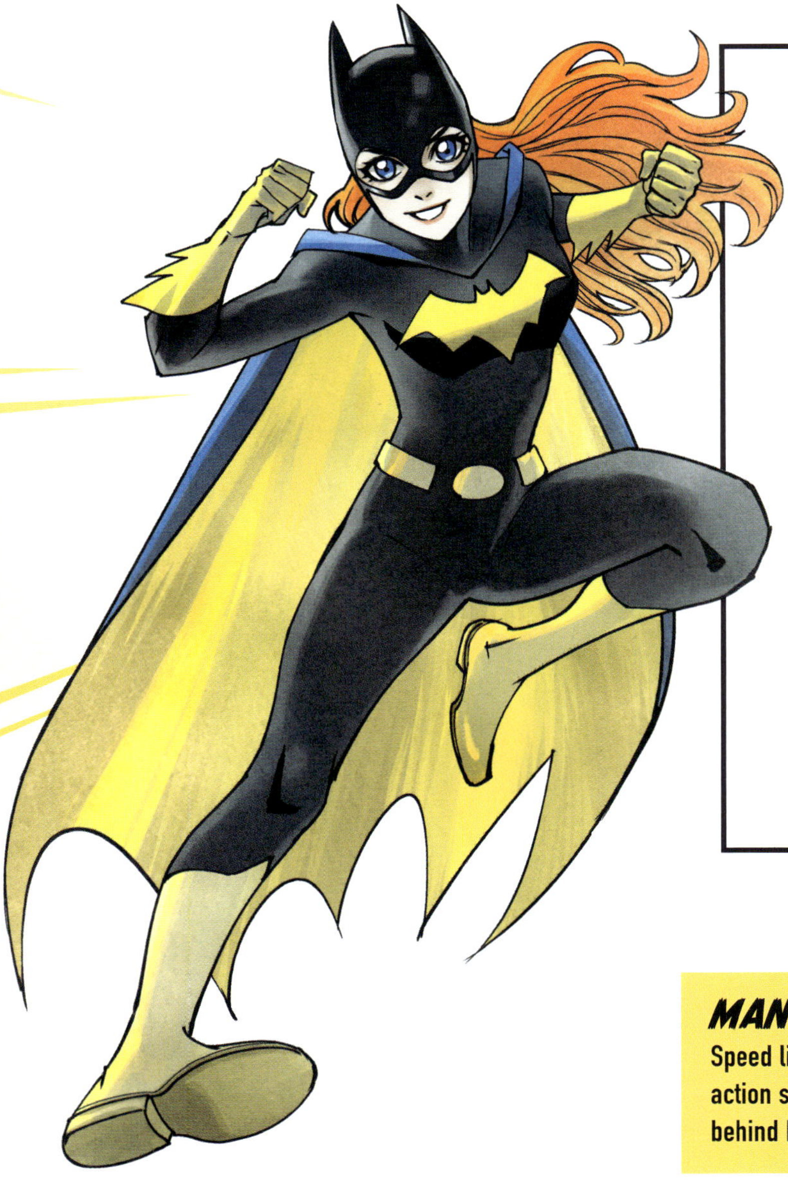

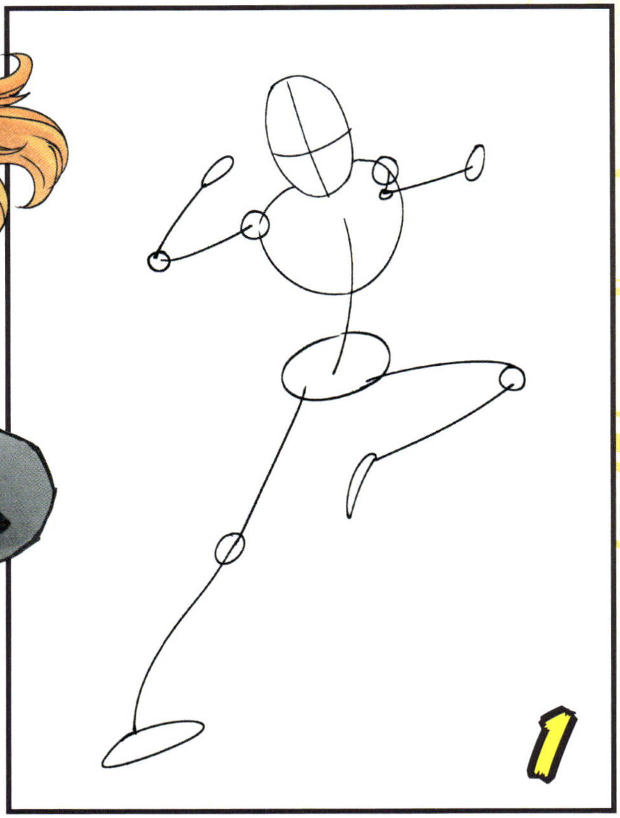
1

MANGA FACT

Speed lines often surround manga characters during action scenes to add excitement. Draw speed lines behind Batgirl to give her kick extra oomph!

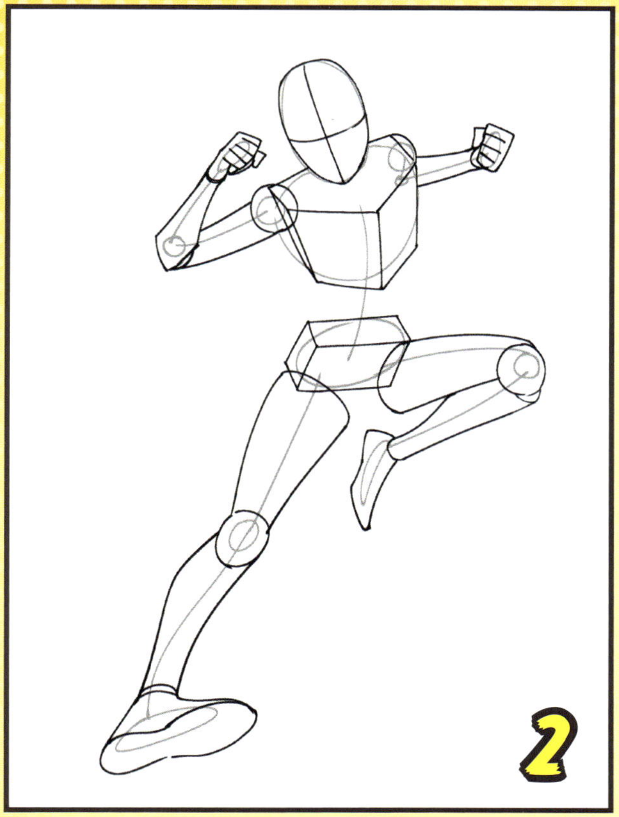
2
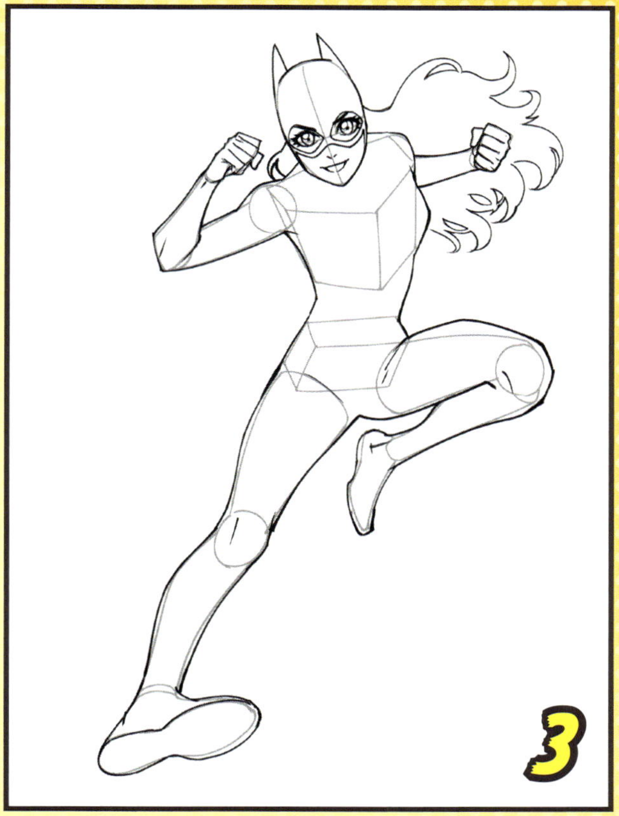
3
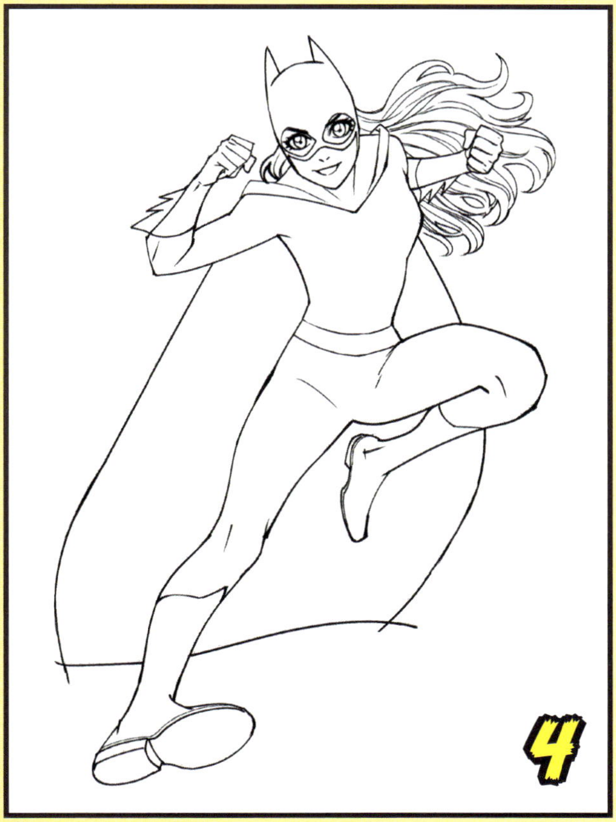
4
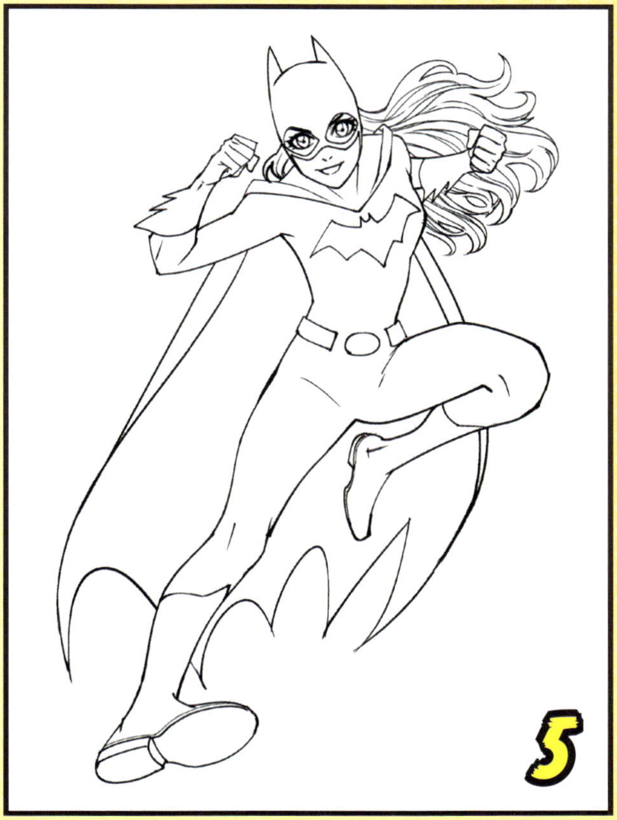
5

BATWING

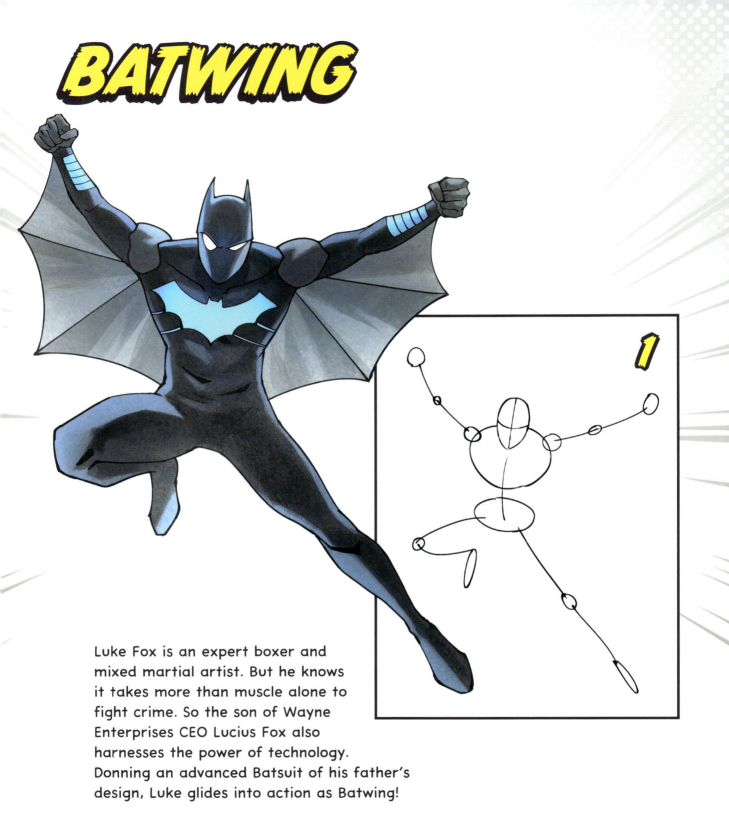

Luke Fox is an expert boxer and mixed martial artist. But he knows it takes more than muscle alone to fight crime. So the son of Wayne Enterprises CEO Lucius Fox also harnesses the power of technology. Donning an advanced Batsuit of his father's design, Luke glides into action as Batwing!

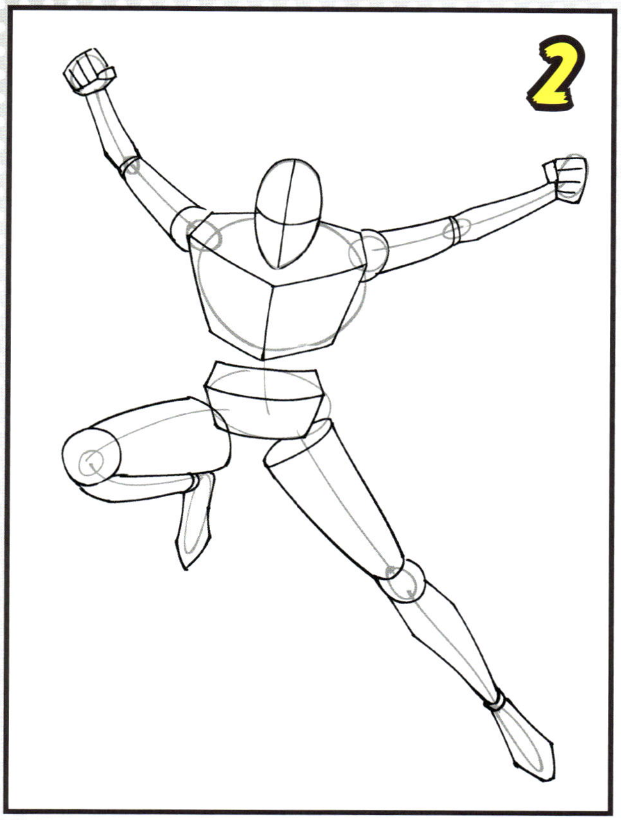
2
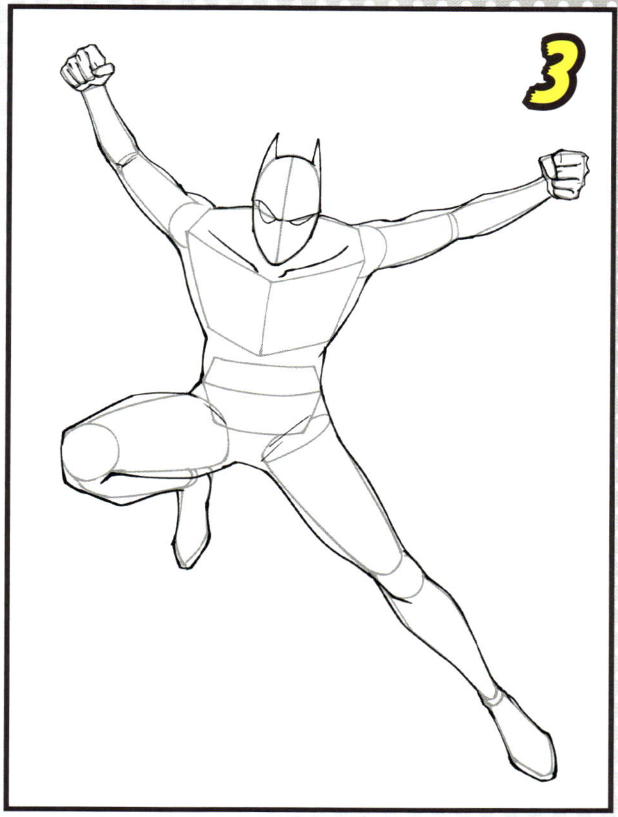
3
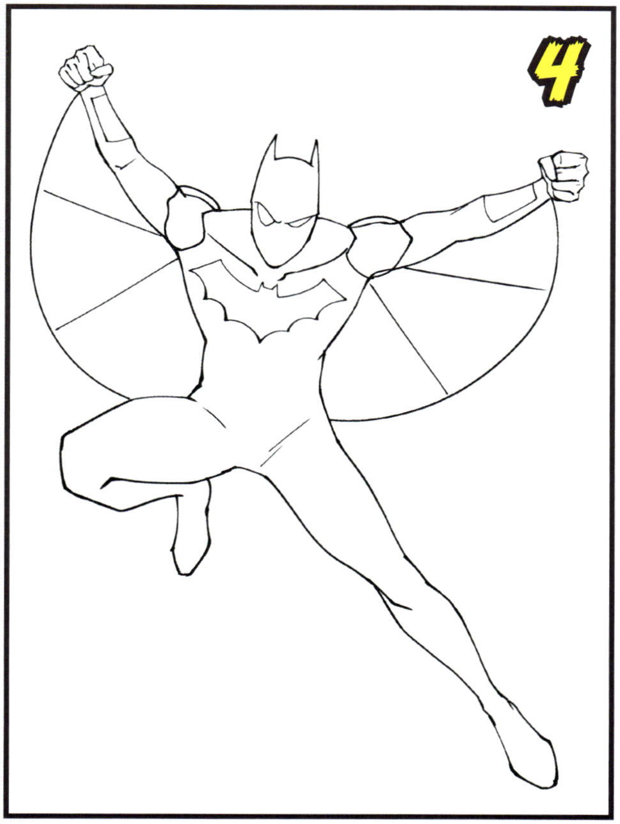
4
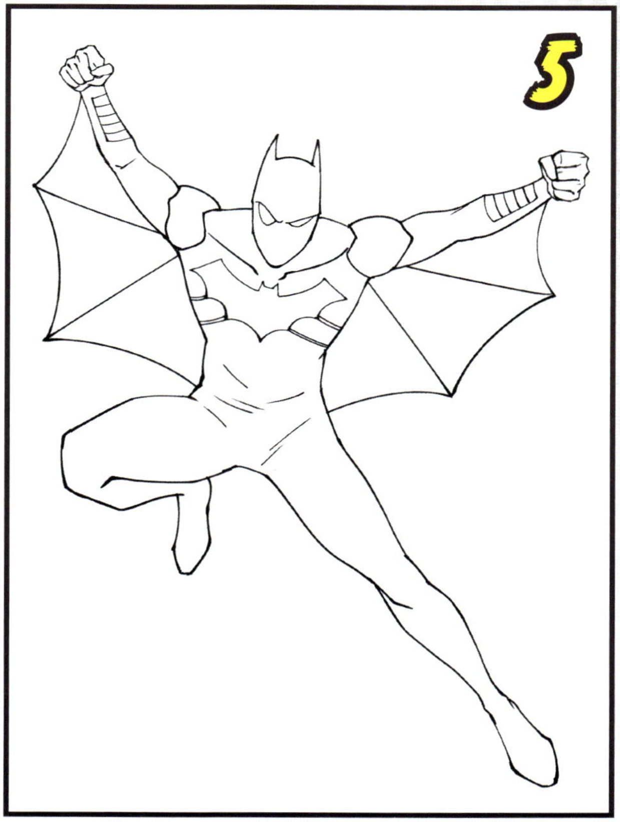
5

BATWOMAN

Kate Kane proves crime fighting runs in the family—the Bat Family. She's a cousin of Bruce Wayne, aka Batman. She's also a dedicated defender of Gotham City. Disguised as Batwoman, she relies on her keen mind and superior combat skills every time she charges fearlessly into a fight!

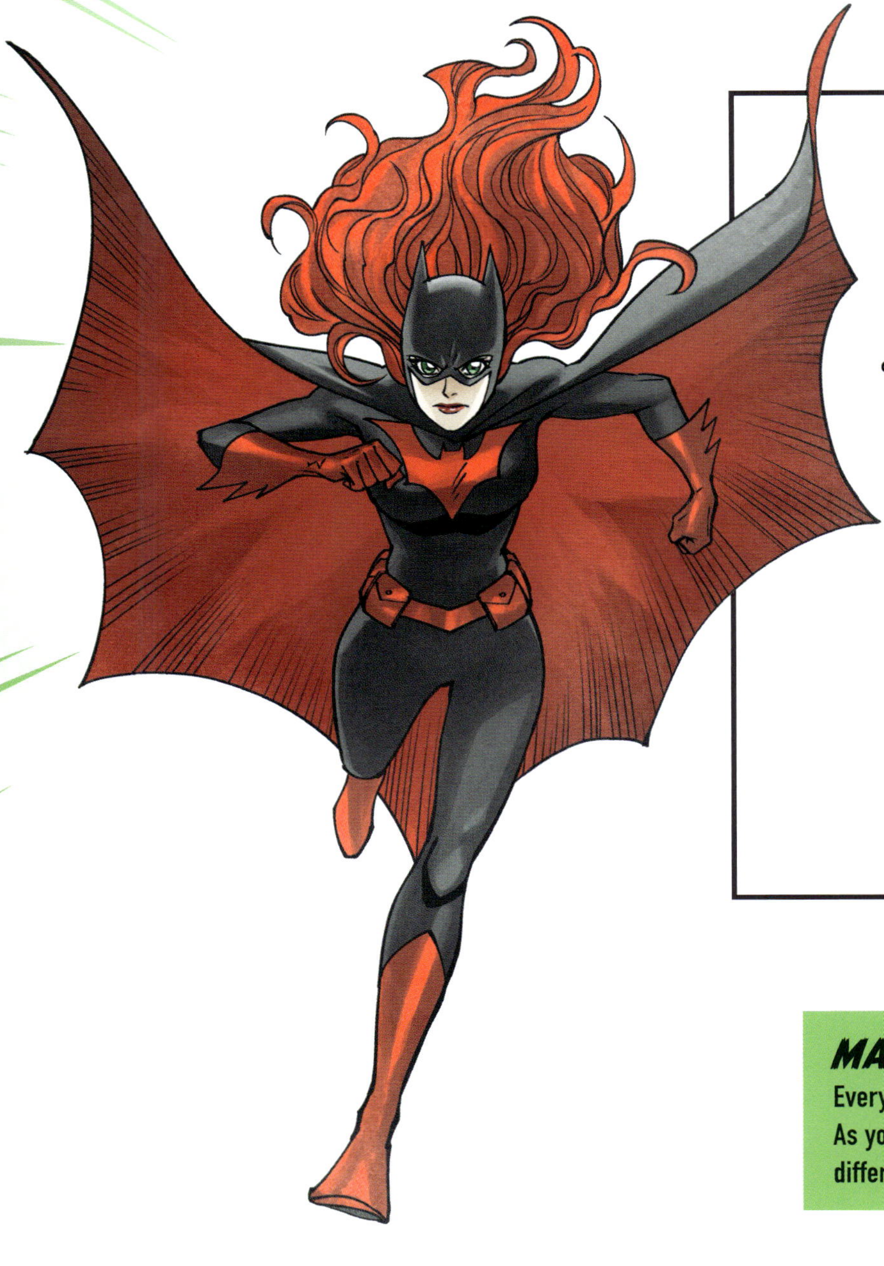

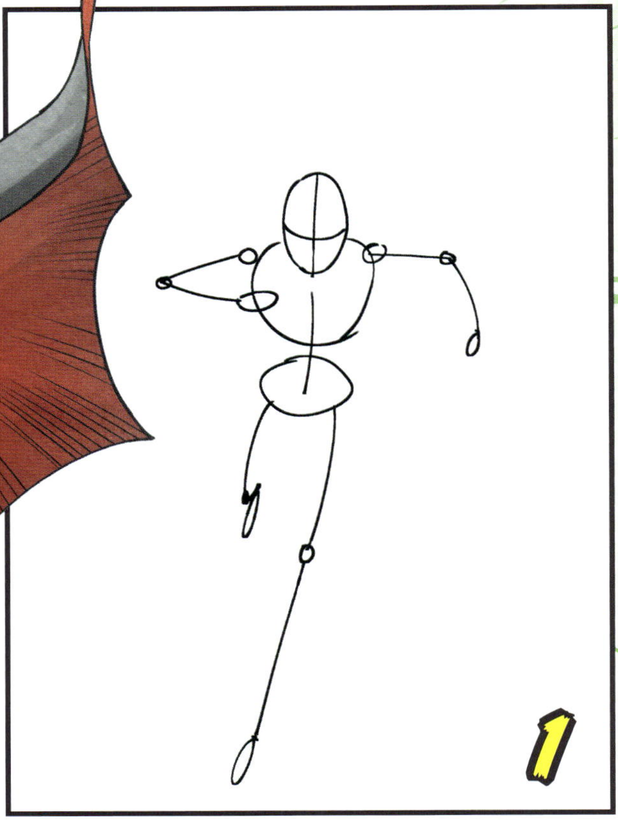
1

MANGA FACT

Every mangaka has their own unique style. As you practice your drawing skills, explore different styles to see which one suits you best.

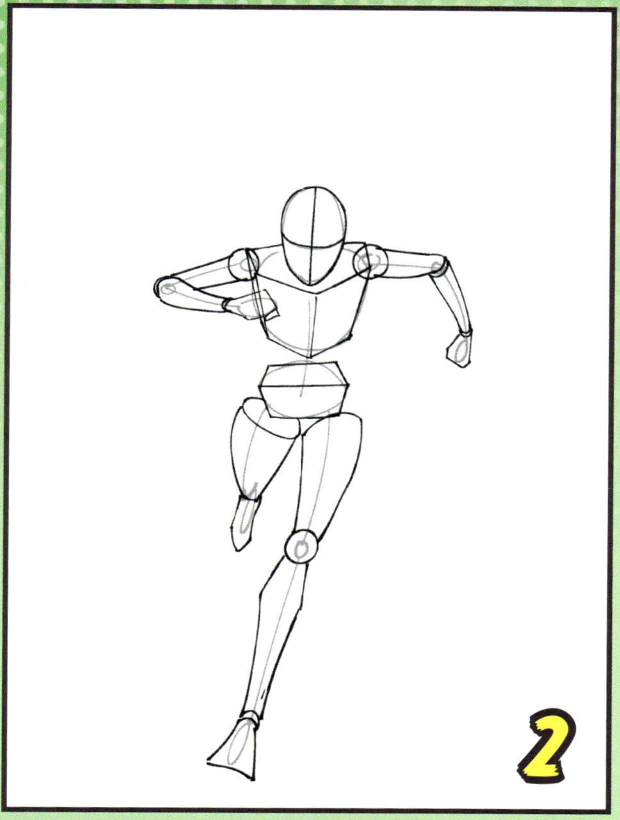
2
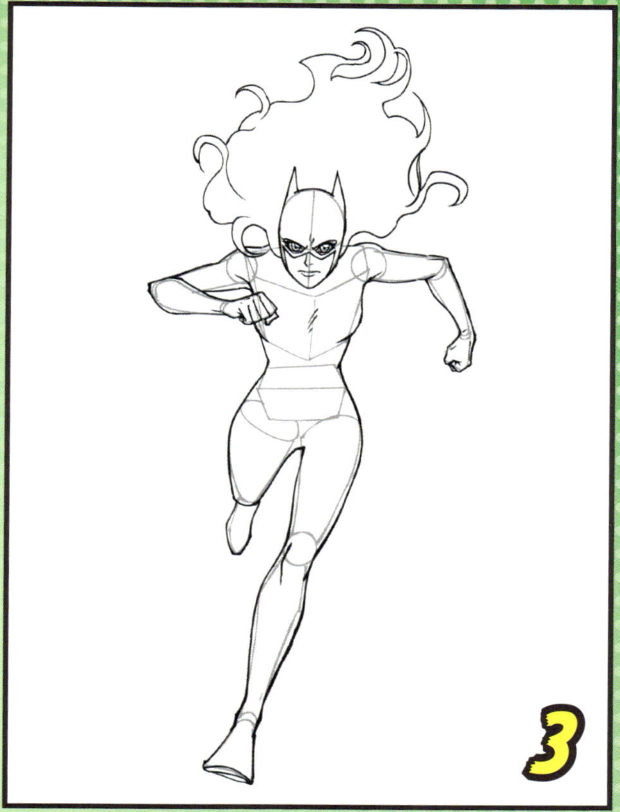
3
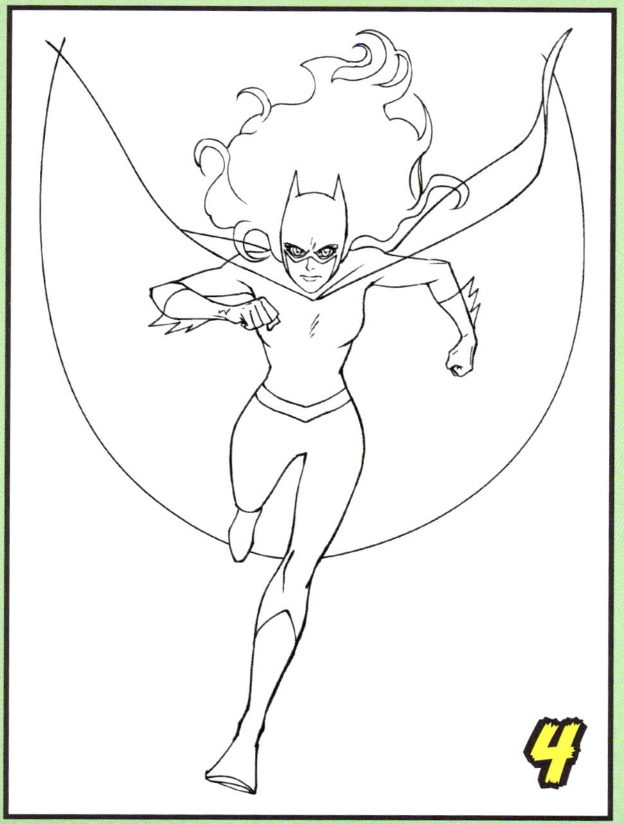
4
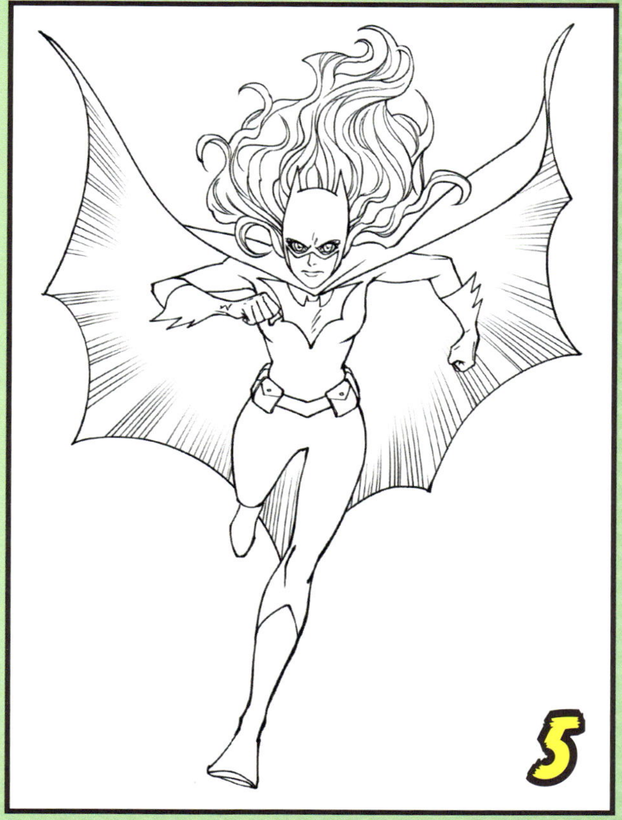
5

CATWOMAN

This professional thief is a bit of a *purr*-fectionist. With feline grace and agility, Catwoman can slink her way into just about any museum gallery or bank vault. But don't think that cracking safes is her only skill. She's also a cunning fighter who isn't afraid to crack her whip!

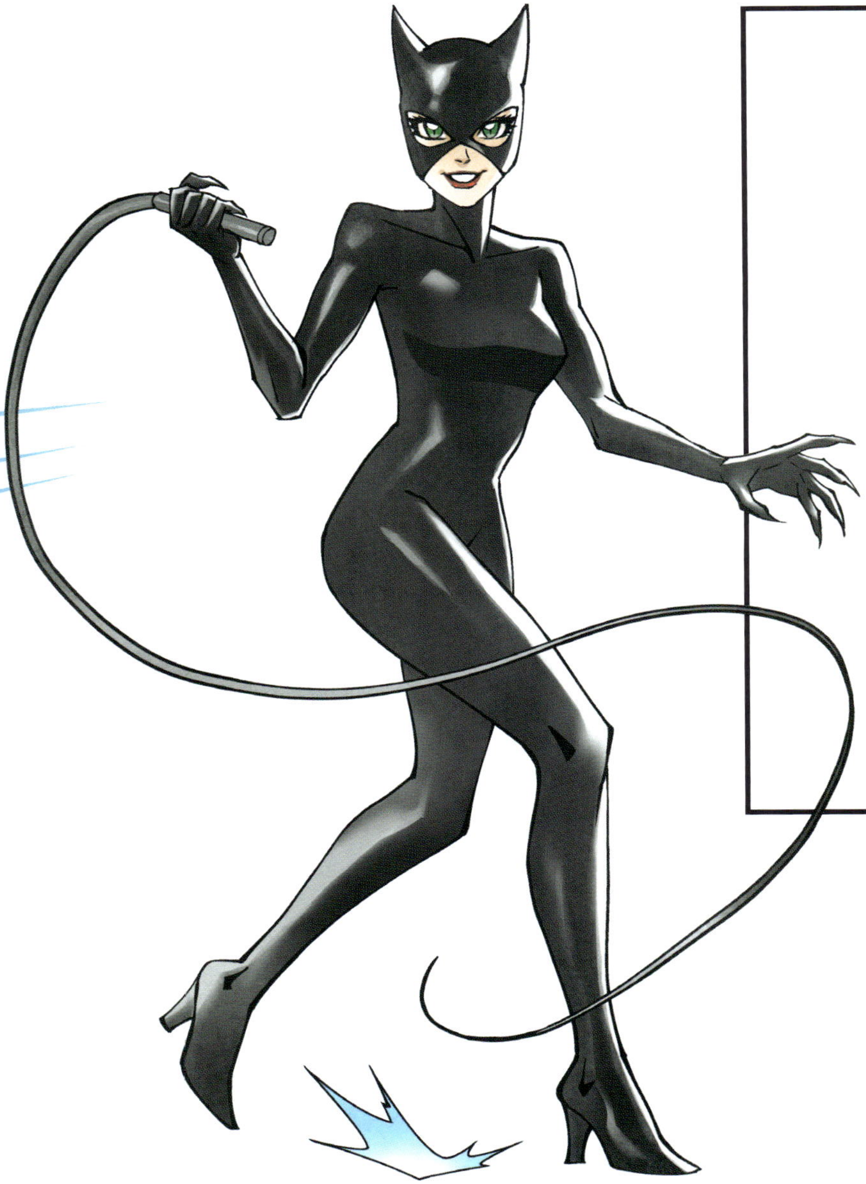

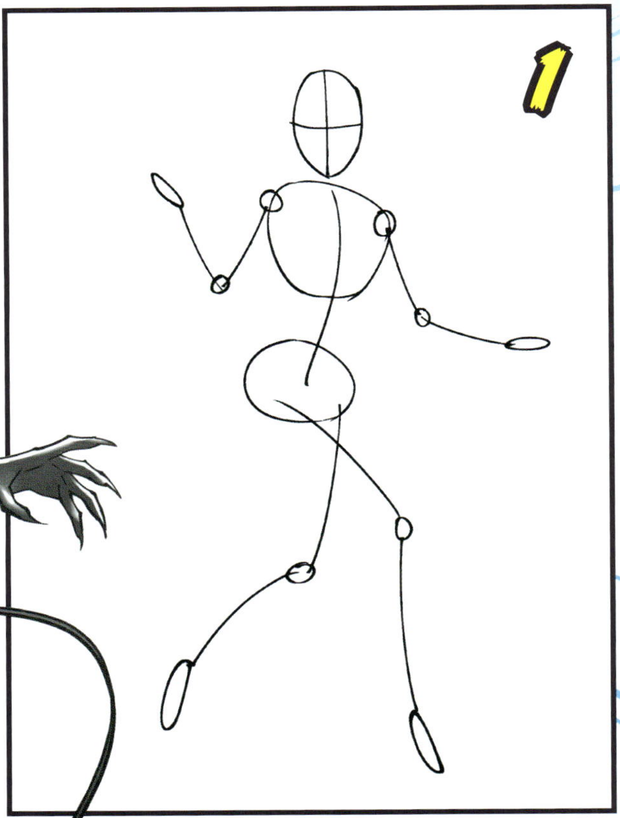
1

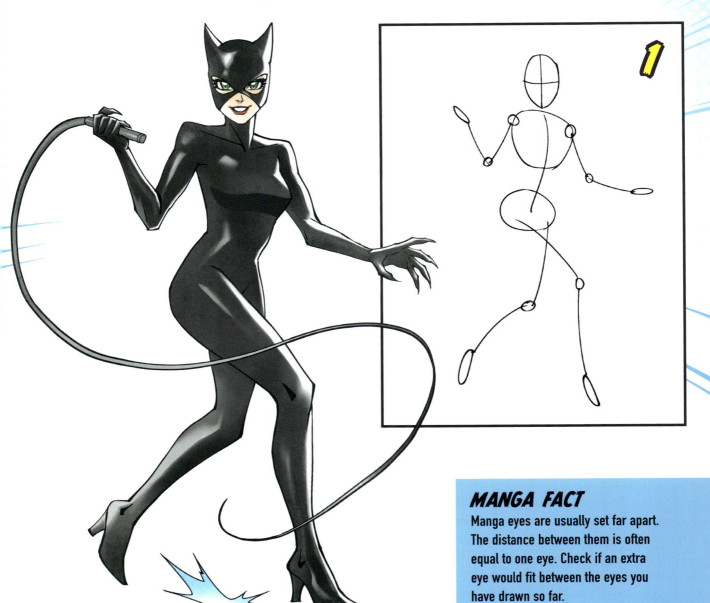

MANGA FACT

Manga eyes are usually set far apart. The distance between them is often equal to one eye. Check if an extra eye would fit between the eyes you have drawn so far.

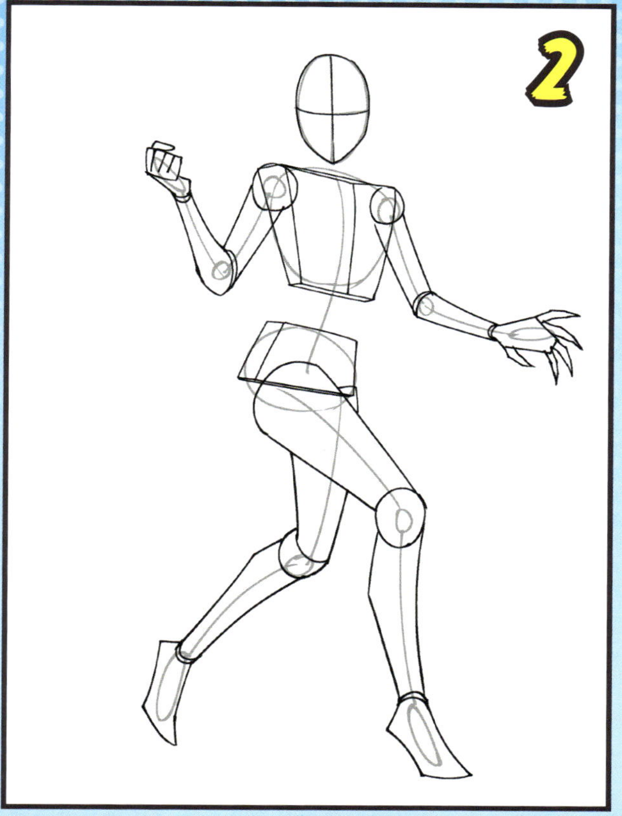
2
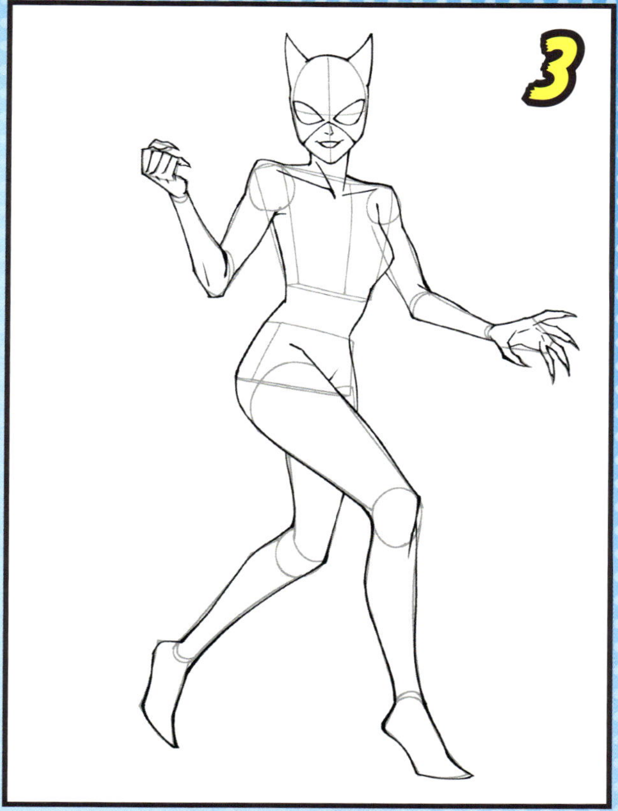
3
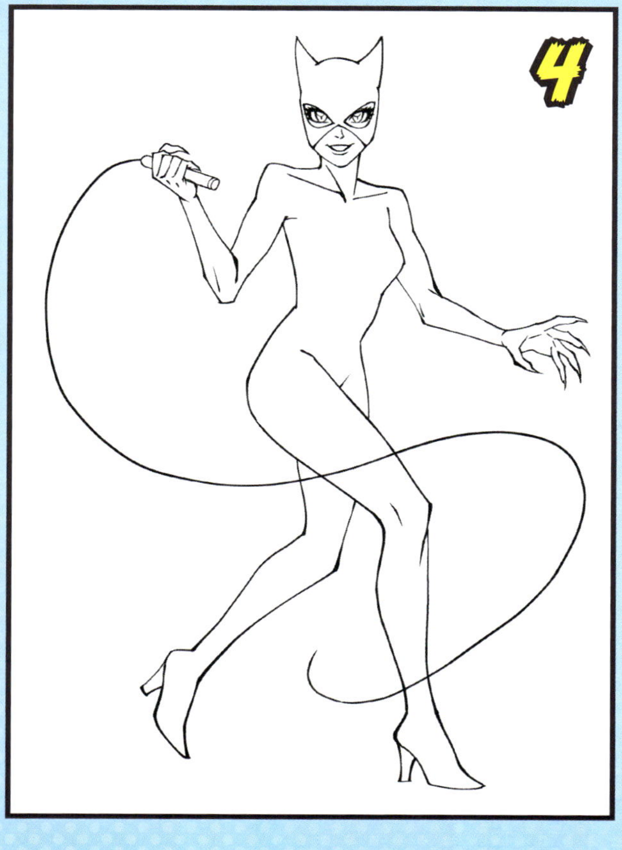
4
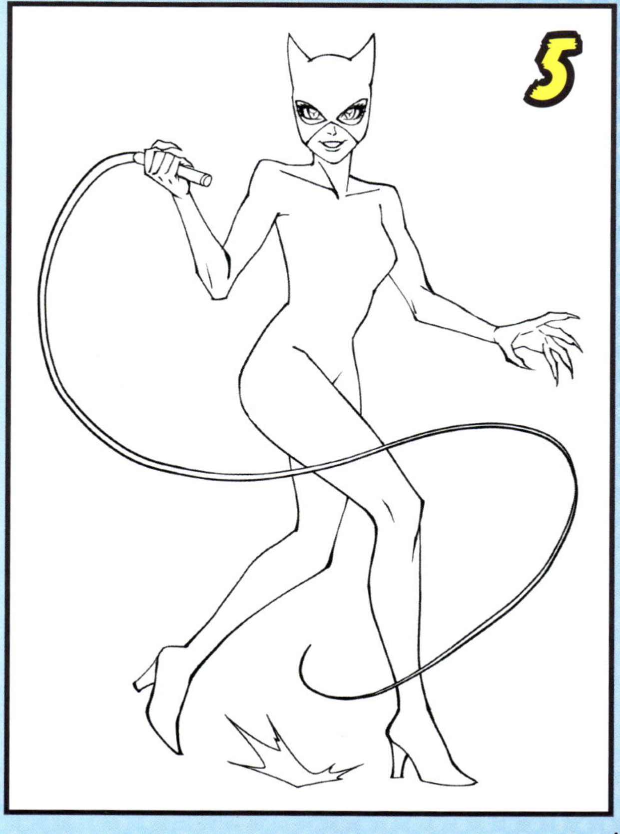
5

THE JOKER

The Joker is Batman's greatest enemy—and a treacherous trickster. From Joker Toxin in his lapel flower to a shocking hand buzzer, the Clown Prince of Crime always has a trick up his sleeve. So look out! Those playing cards are as razor-sharp as his criminal mind!

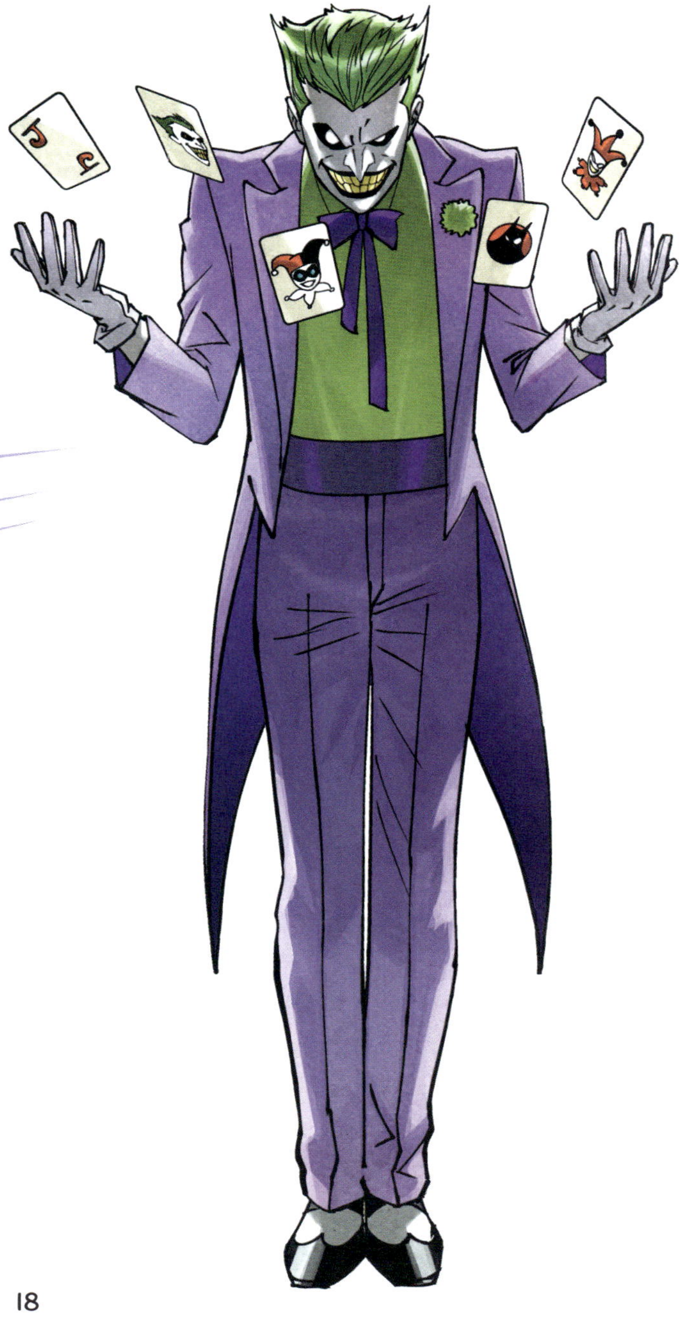

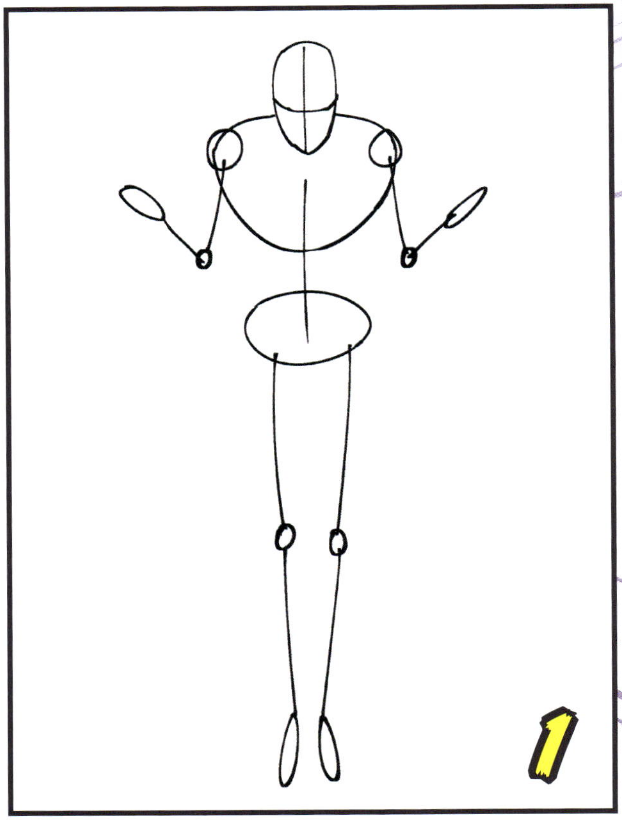
1

MANGA FACT

In Japan, shōnen manga is geared toward boys. Shōjo manga is aimed at girls. But boys and girls often read both.

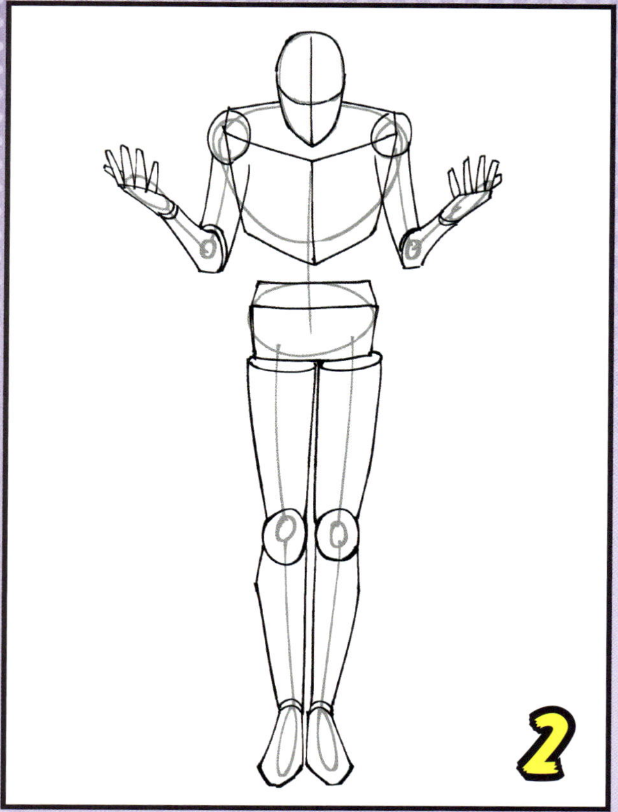
2
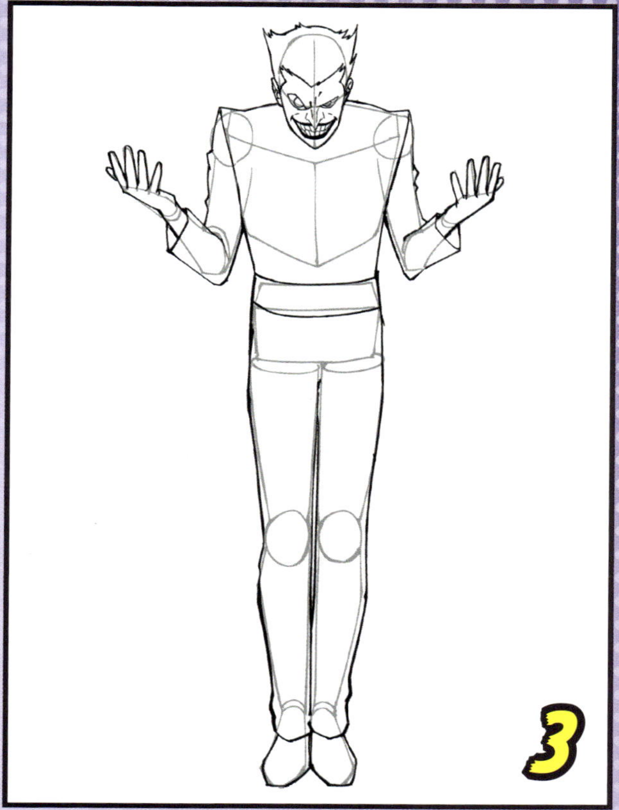
3
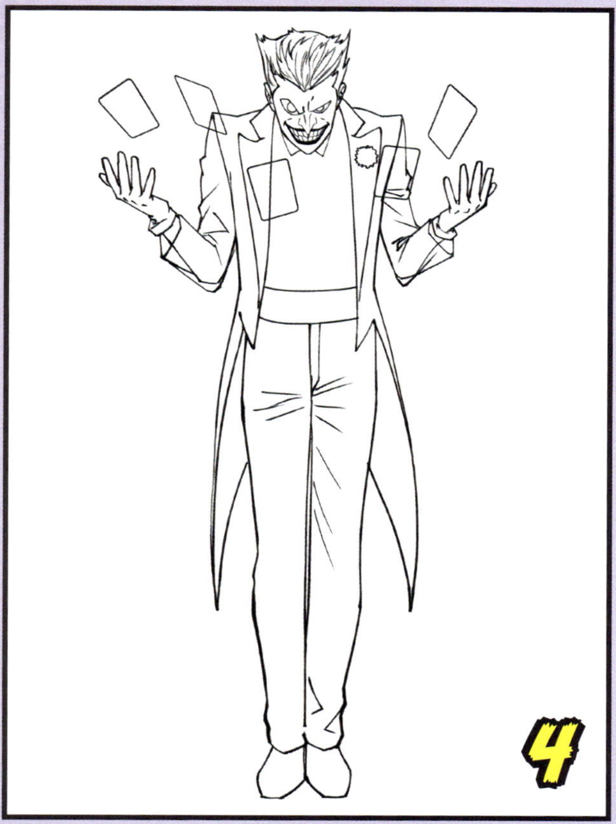
4
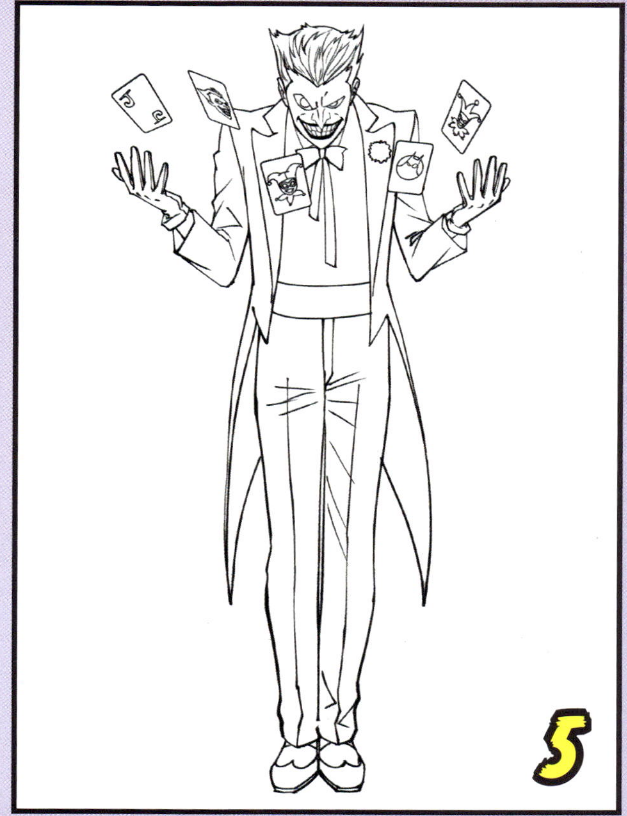
5

HARLEY QUINN

Harley Quinn may be a jester, but she's nobody's fool. The Clown Princess of Crime knows what she wants—lots and lots of moolah! And you can bet she's going to have a hoot while grabbing the loot. With her huge mallet in hand, Harley has a smashing good time!

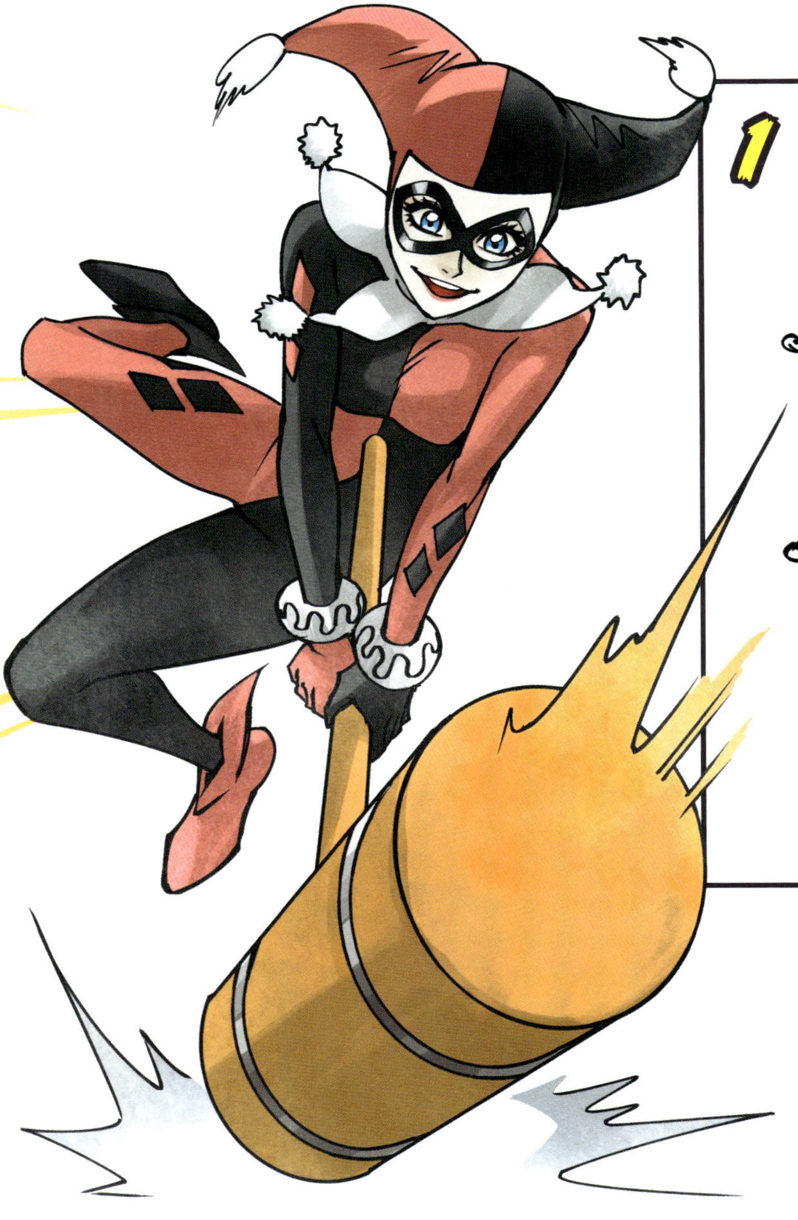

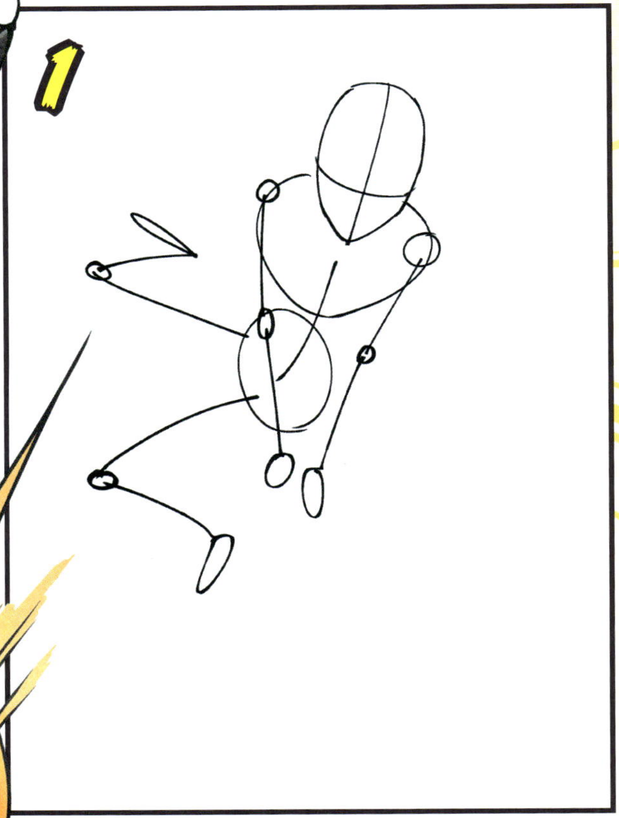
1

MANGA FACT

Chibis are short, cute characters with large heads and tiny bodies. Imagine Harley as a chibi and try drawing her in that style!

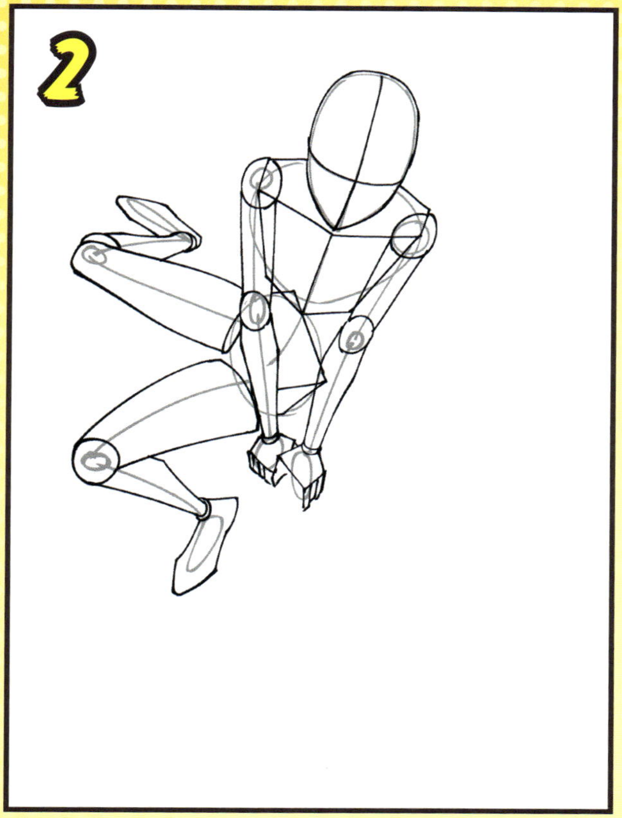
2
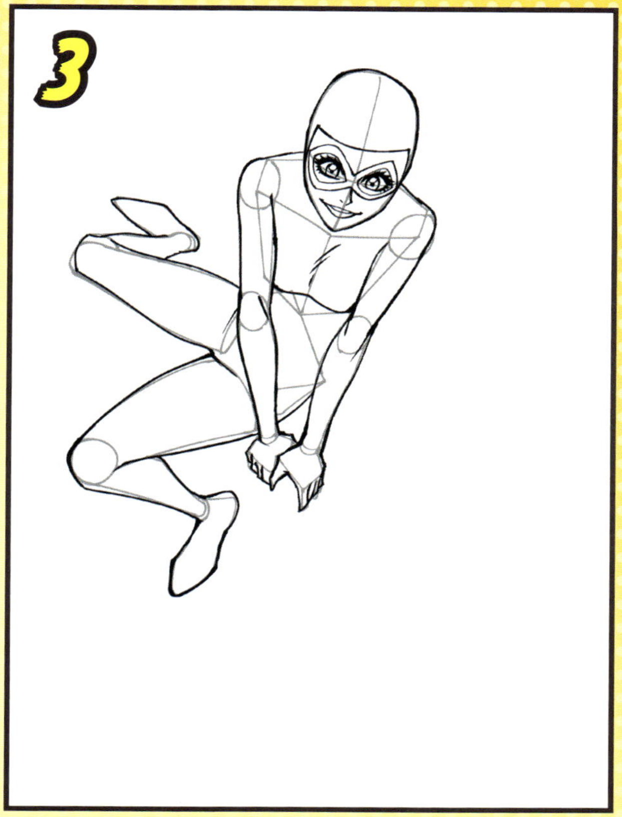
3
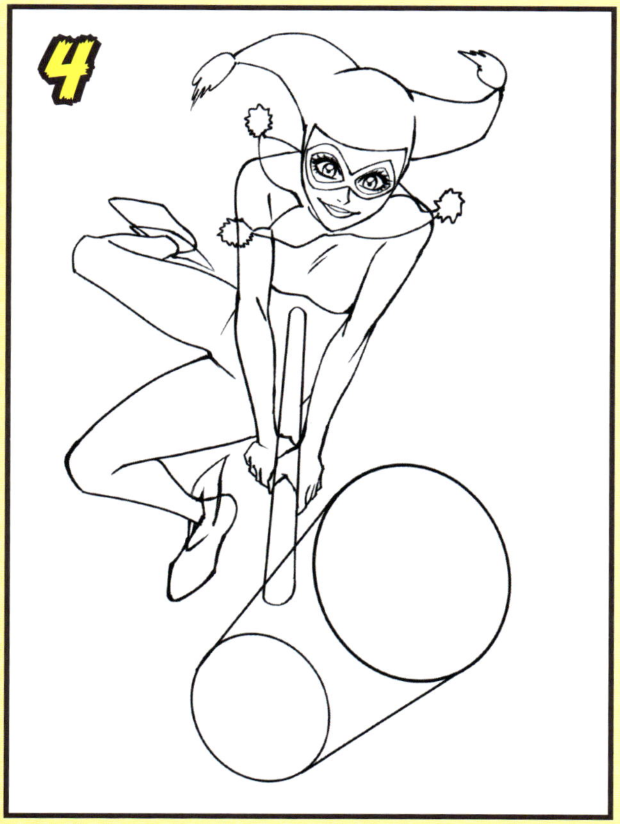
4
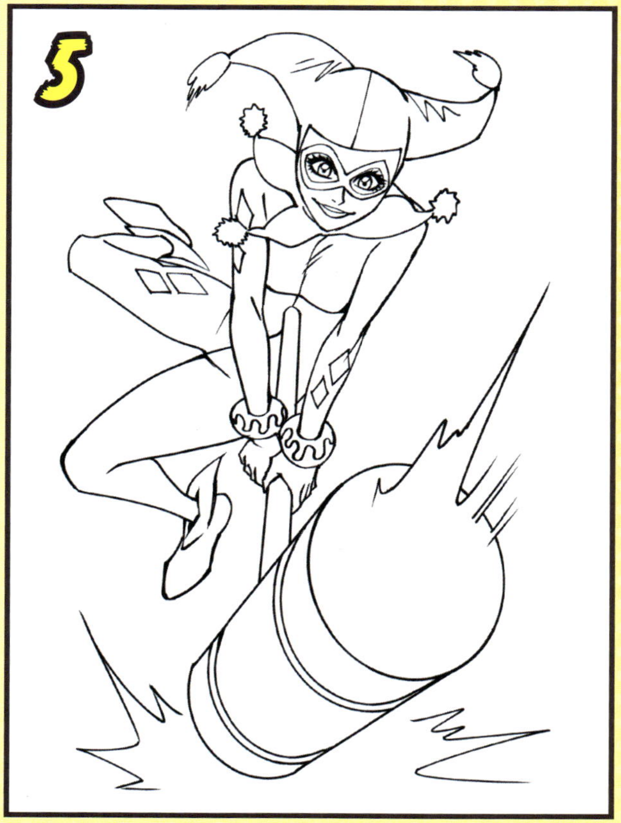
5

THE RIDDLER

Why would a cunning criminal leave clever clues for a caped crime fighter to crack? For this rascal of riddles, the answer is elementary: Why not? Armed with his question mark cane and a wily wit, the Riddler loves nothing more than to baffle Batman!

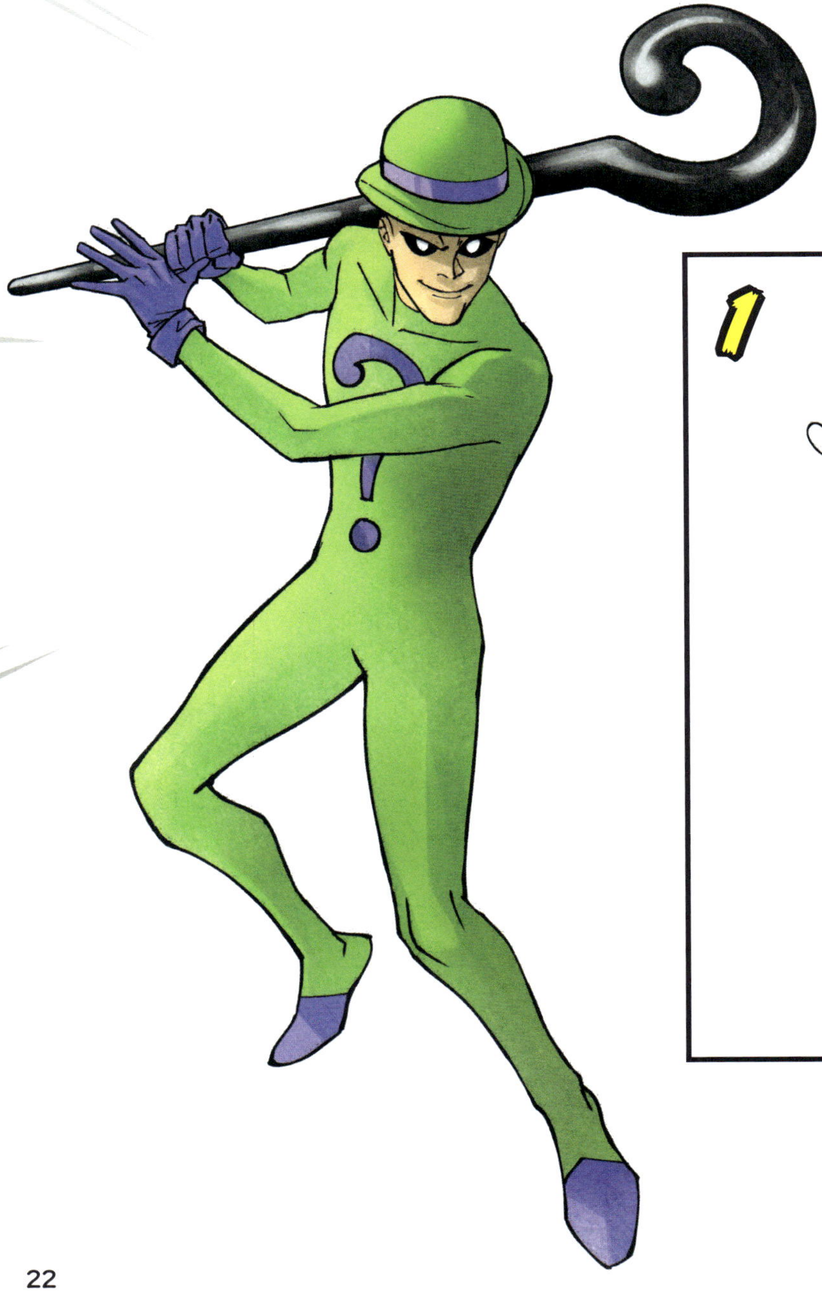

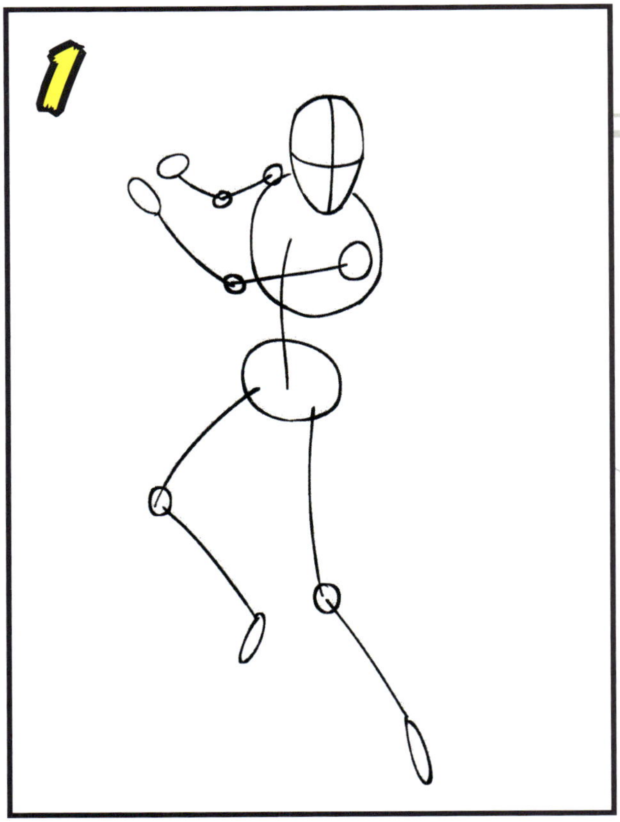
1

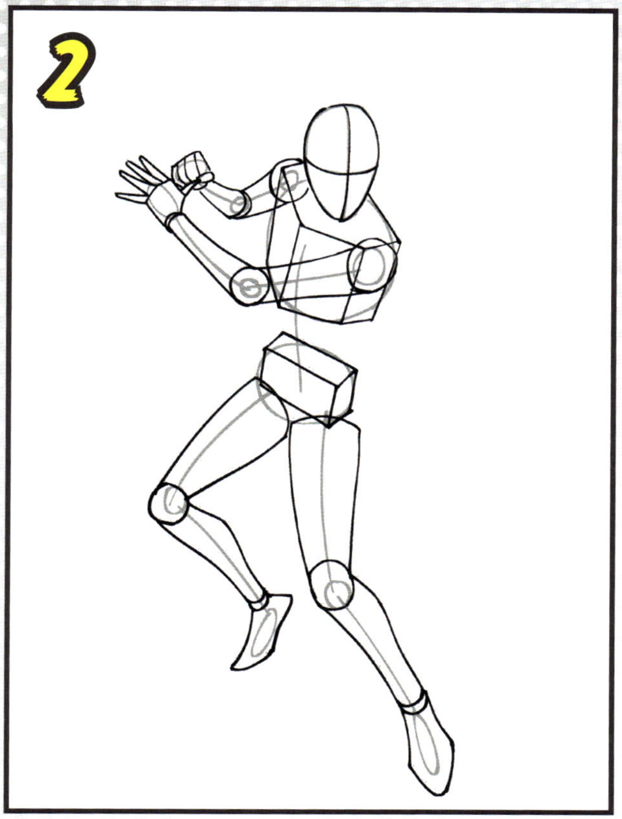
2

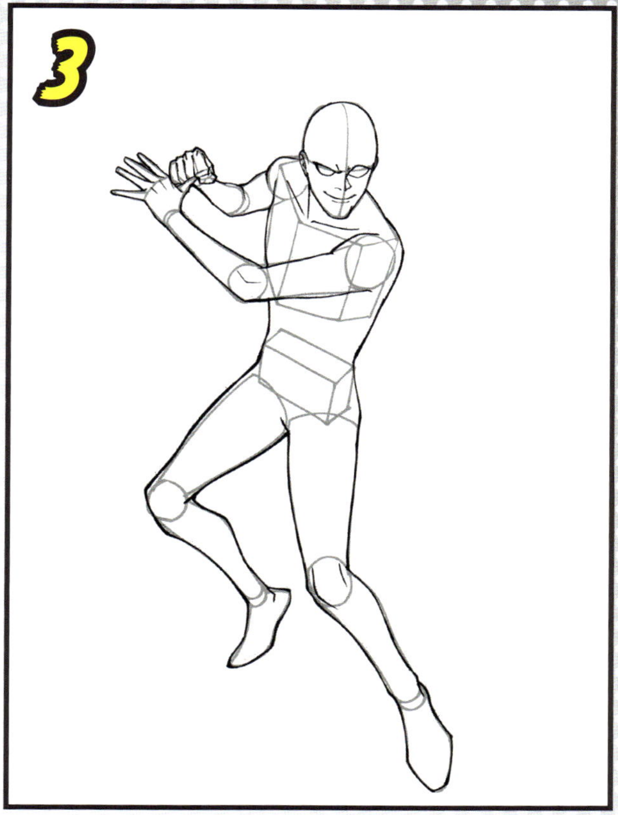
3

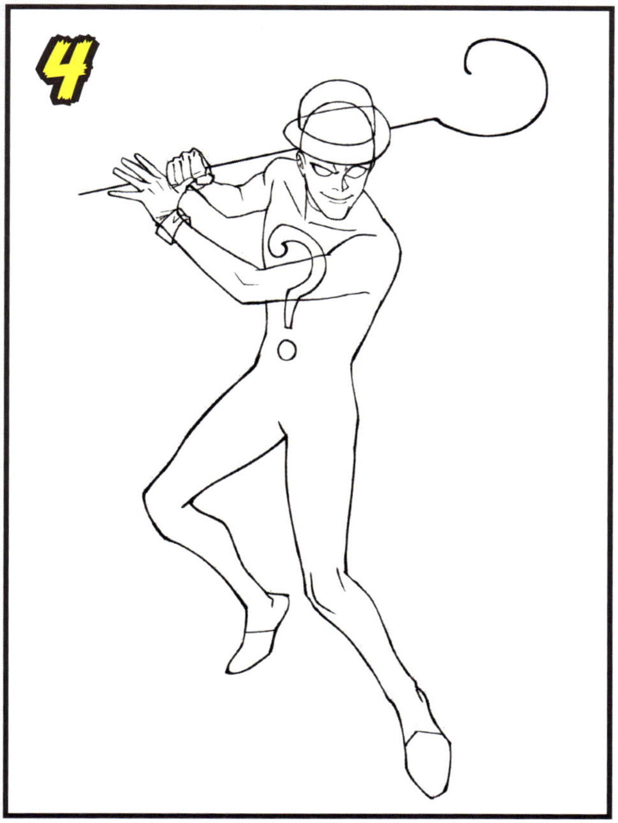
4

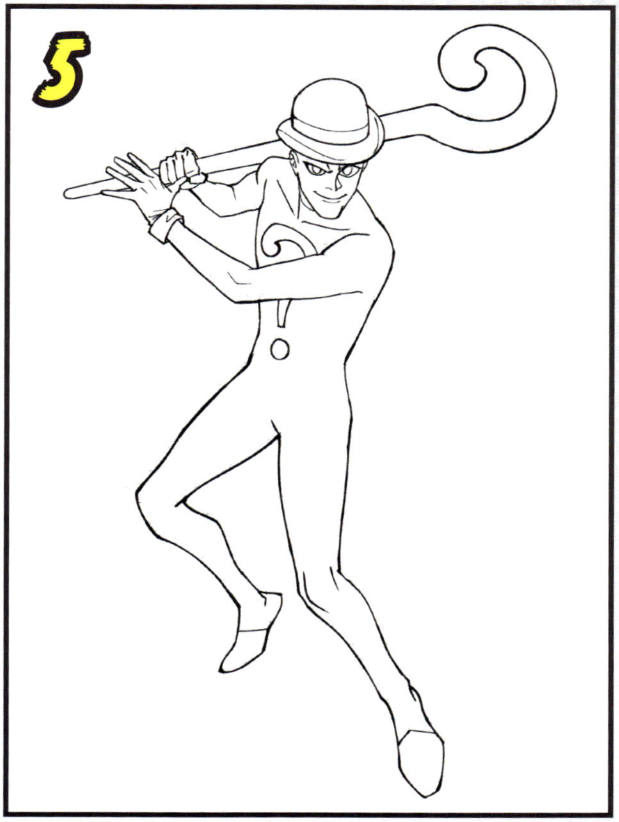
5

POISON IVY

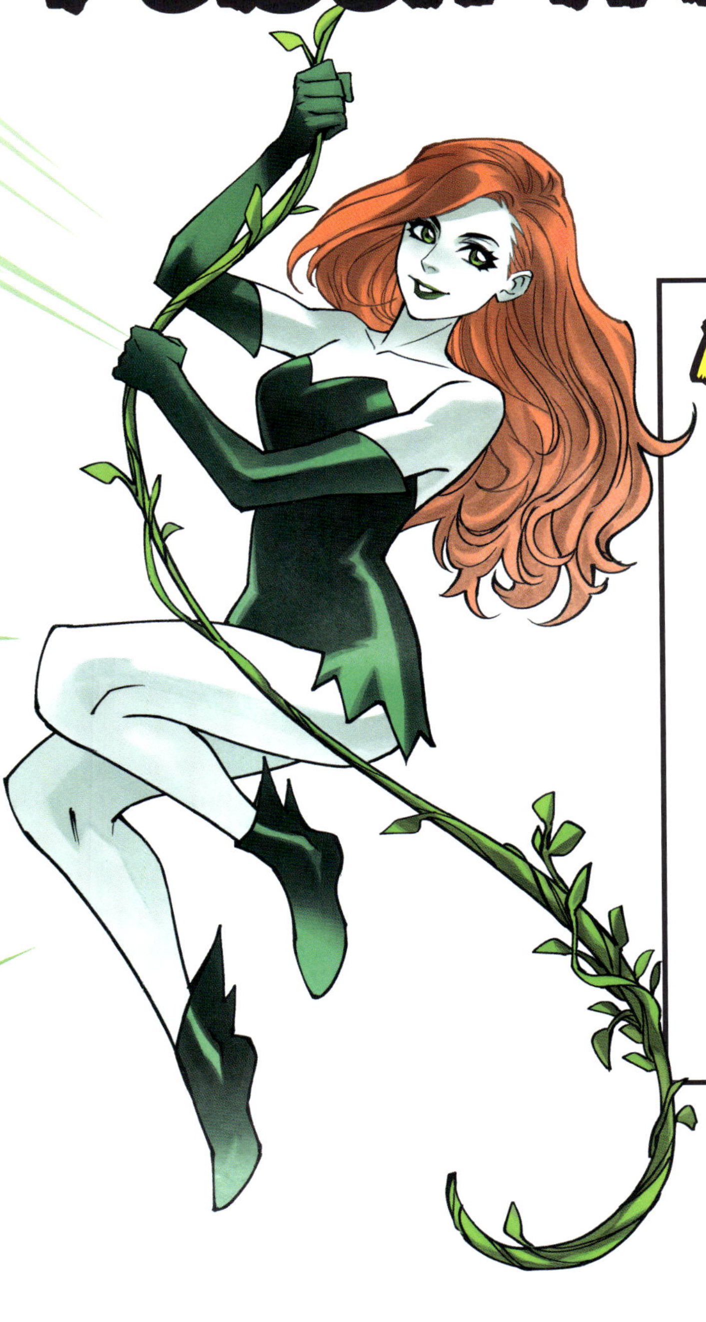

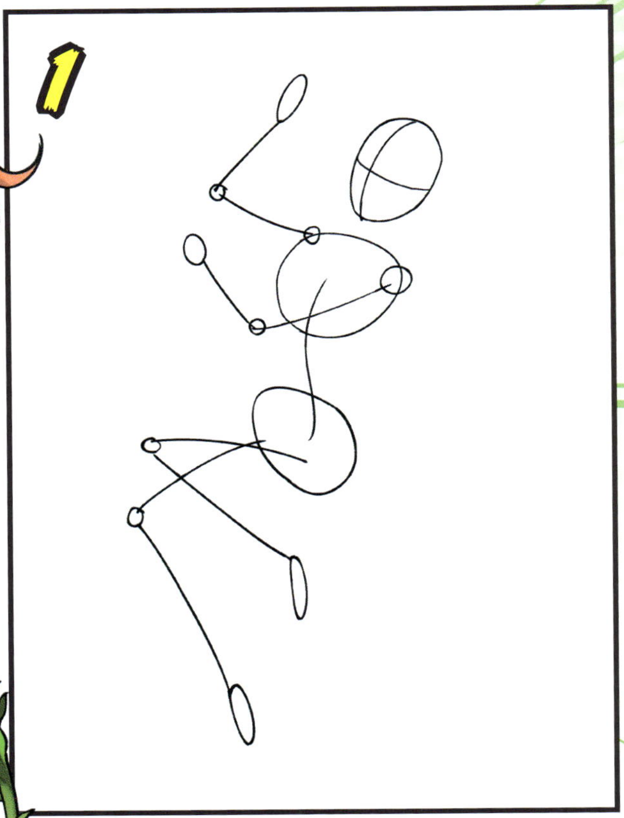
1

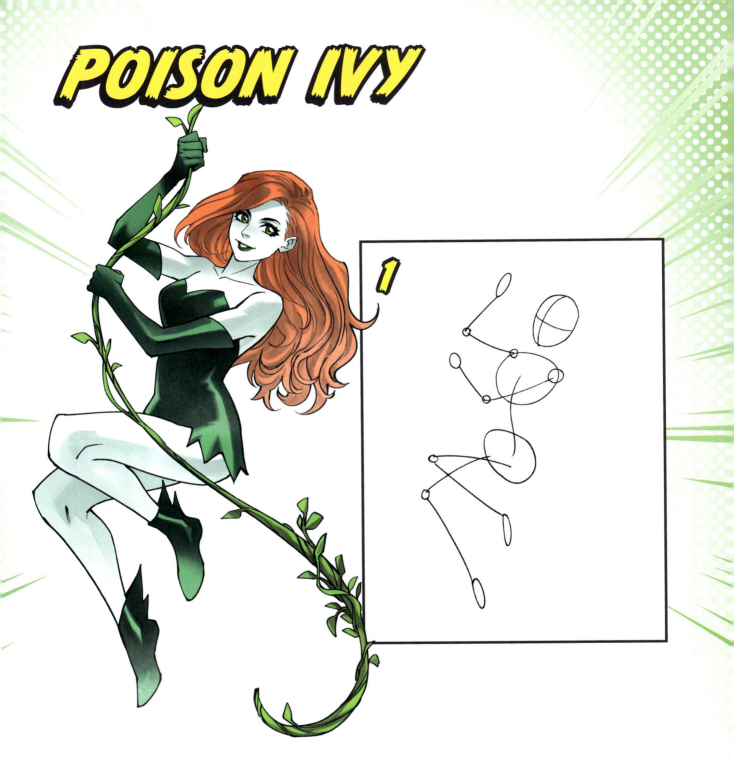

Make way for the Queen of Green! Using just her mind, Poison Ivy commands plants to carry out her wicked whims. From venomous Venus flytraps to vicious vines, this villain's fearsome flora can ensnare even the most daring do-gooders!

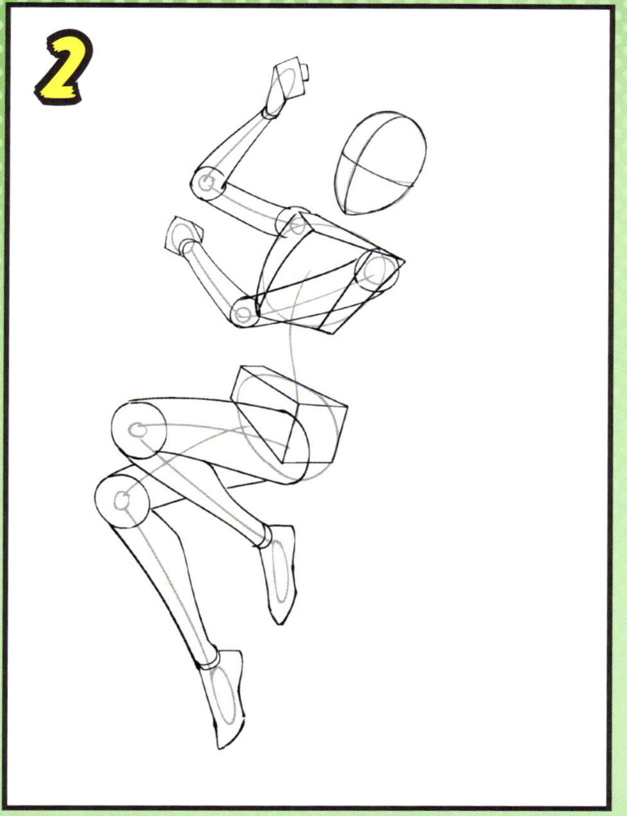
2
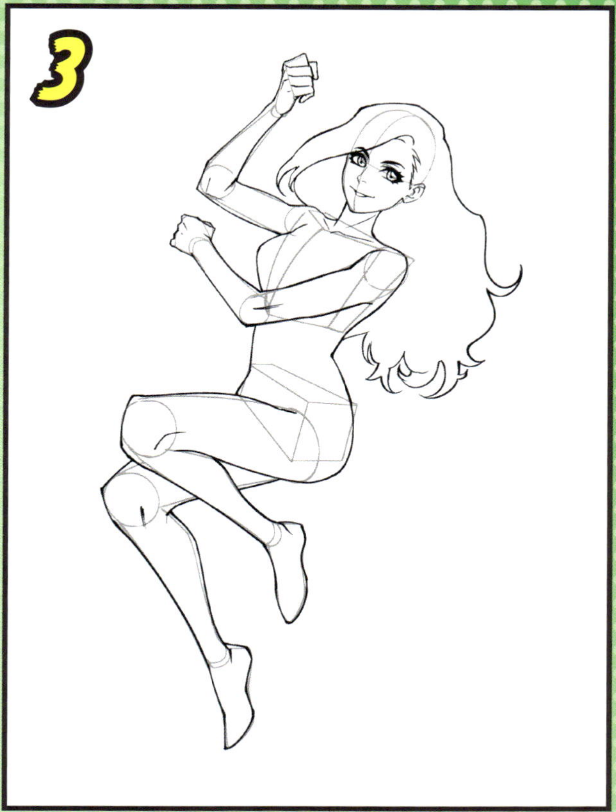
3
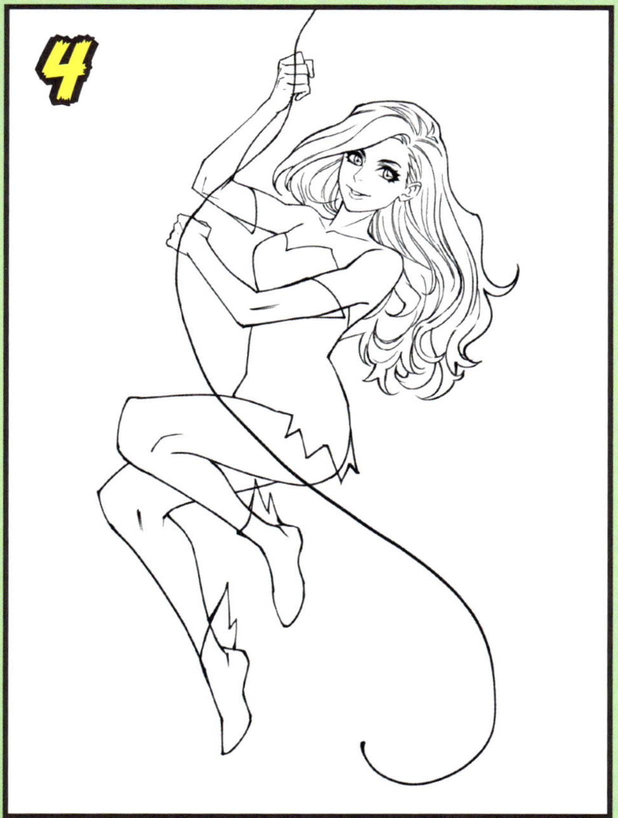
4
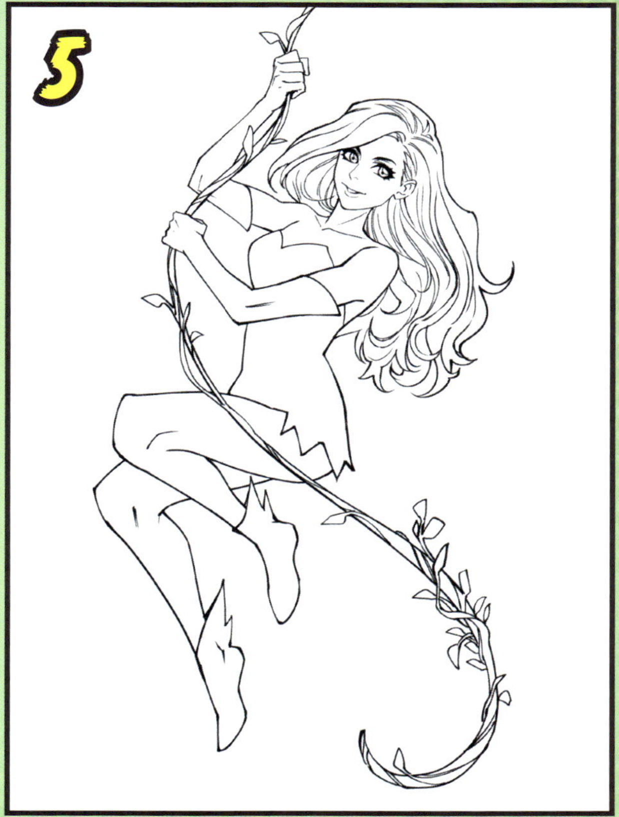
5

THE PENGUIN

The Penguin is a criminal kingpin who's as proud as a peacock. He's always dressed for success when pulling off his plots. With his trademark top hat, monocle, and tuxedo, the self-proclaimed "Gentleman of Crime" certainly looks the part. But beware this bad bird's tricky umbrella—or your goose is cooked!

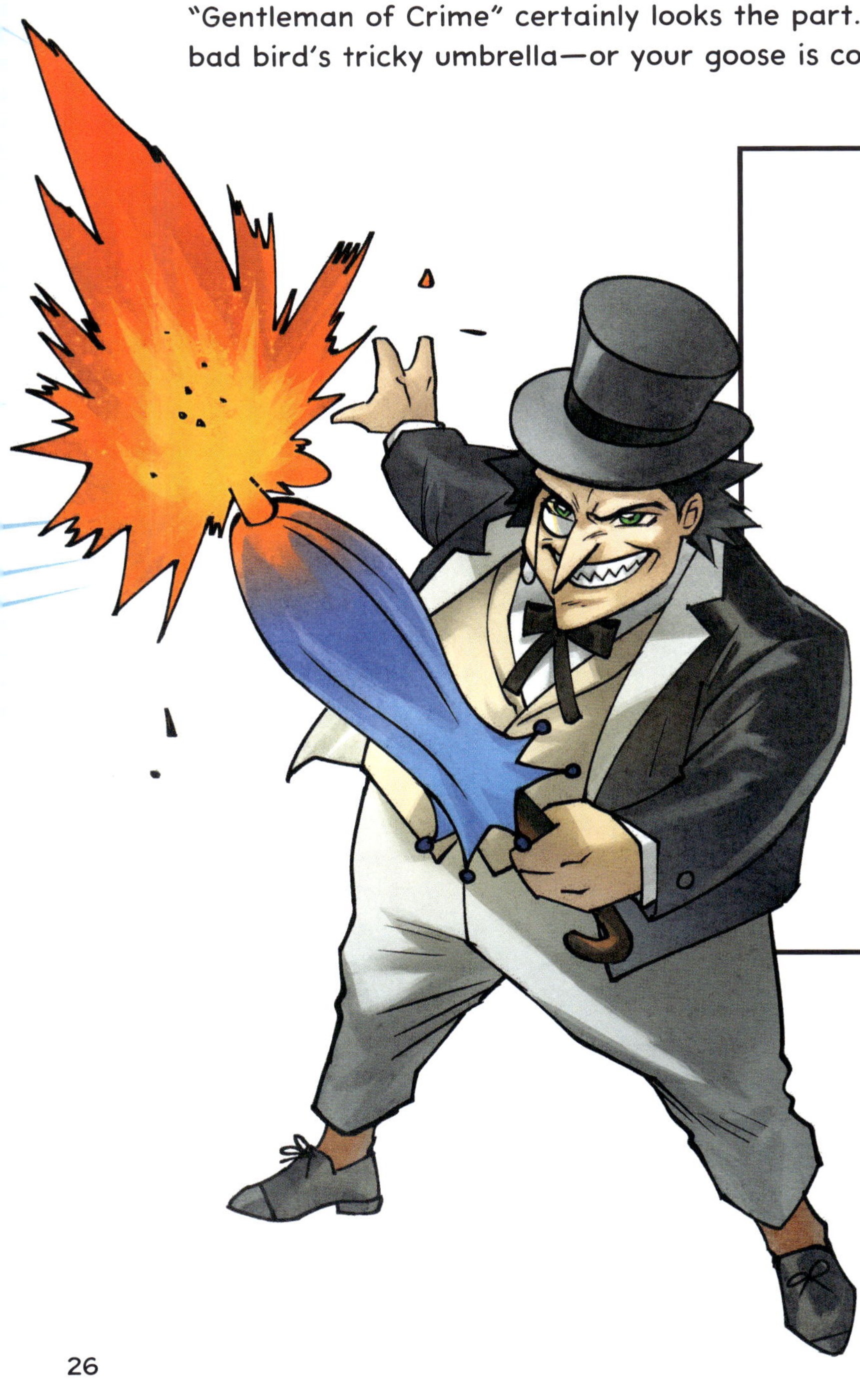

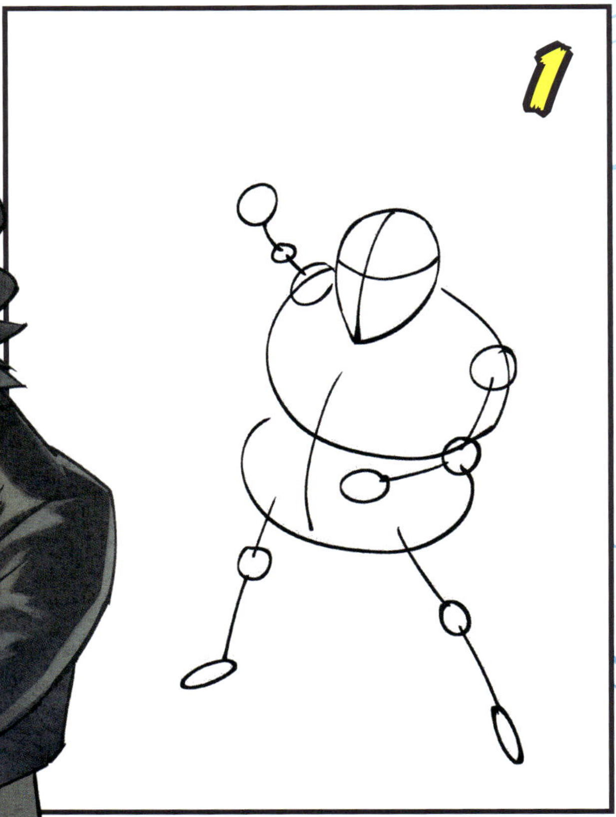
1

MANGA FACT

Manga series feature more than just super heroes and action adventures. From history and sports to fantasy and comedy, manga has many types of stories for everyone to enjoy.

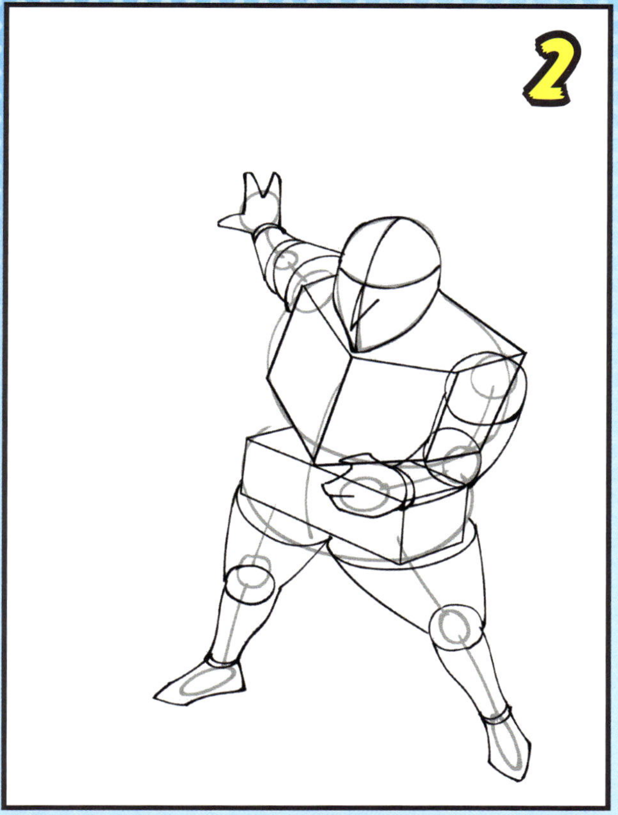
2
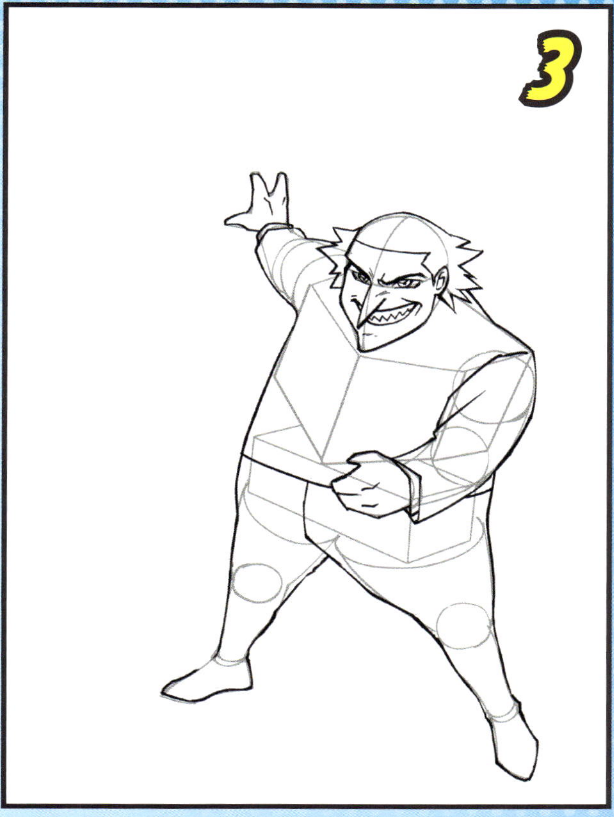
3
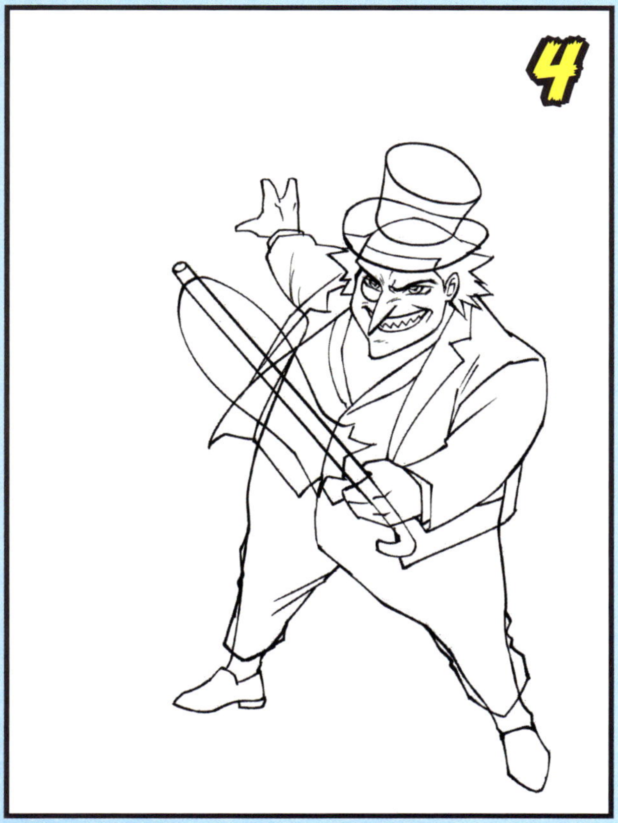
4
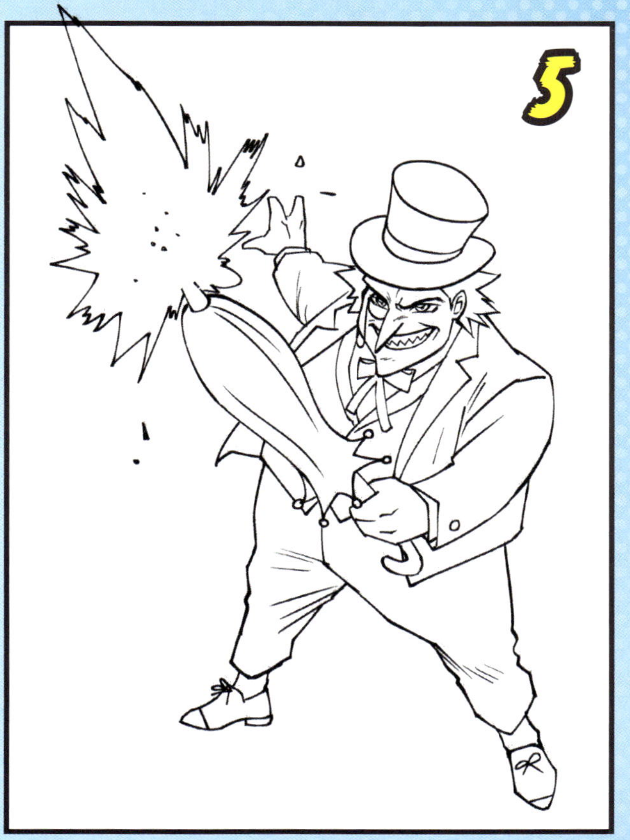
5

BATMAN VS. CLAYFACE

As Clayface rampages through the streets, Batman springs into action. Will the shape-shifting villain's twisted tentacle send the Dark Knight flying? Or can the Caped Crusader bring this muddy menace to justice? AS THE MANGAKA, THE FATE OF GOTHAM CITY IS IN YOUR HANDS!

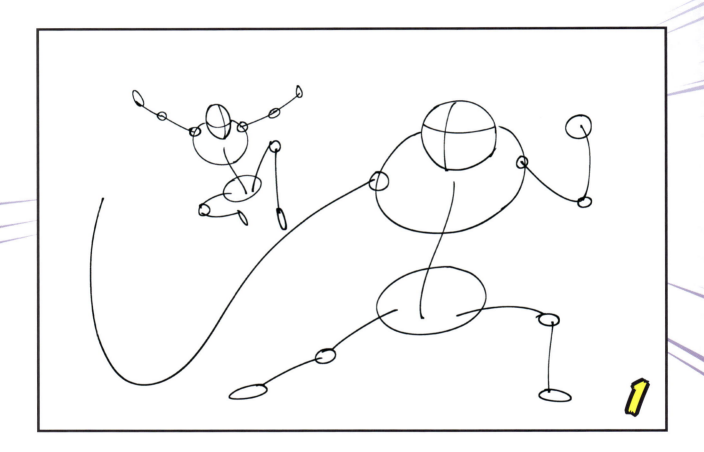

MANGA FACT
Osamu Tezuka is often called the "Godfather of Manga." During his career, he created more than 170,000 pages of manga! *Astro Boy* and *Princess Knight* were among his most popular.

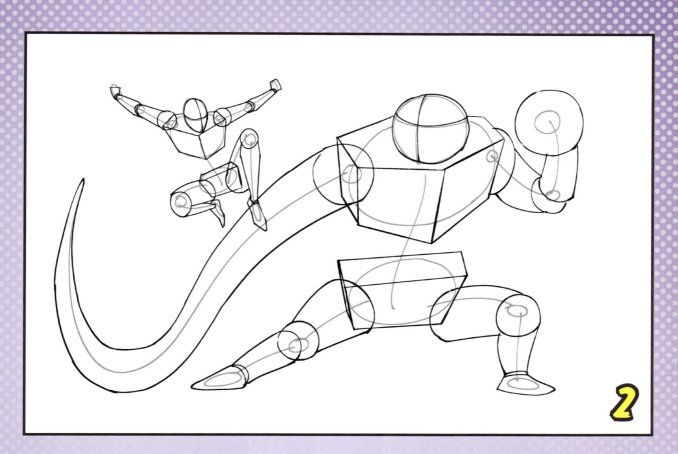

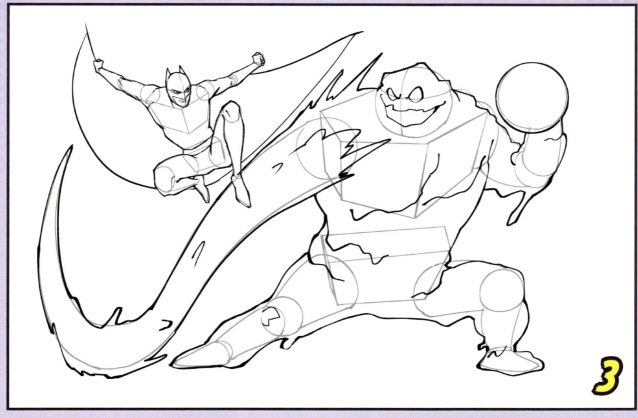

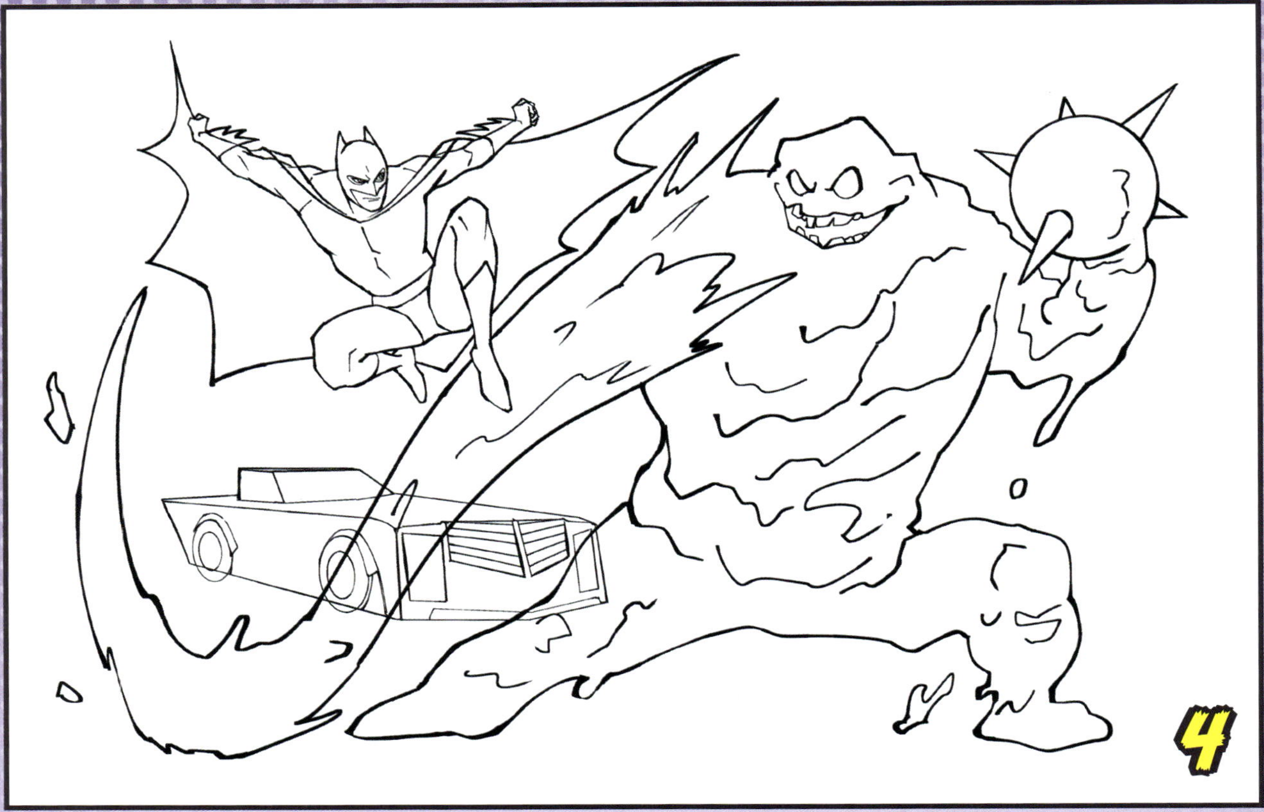
4

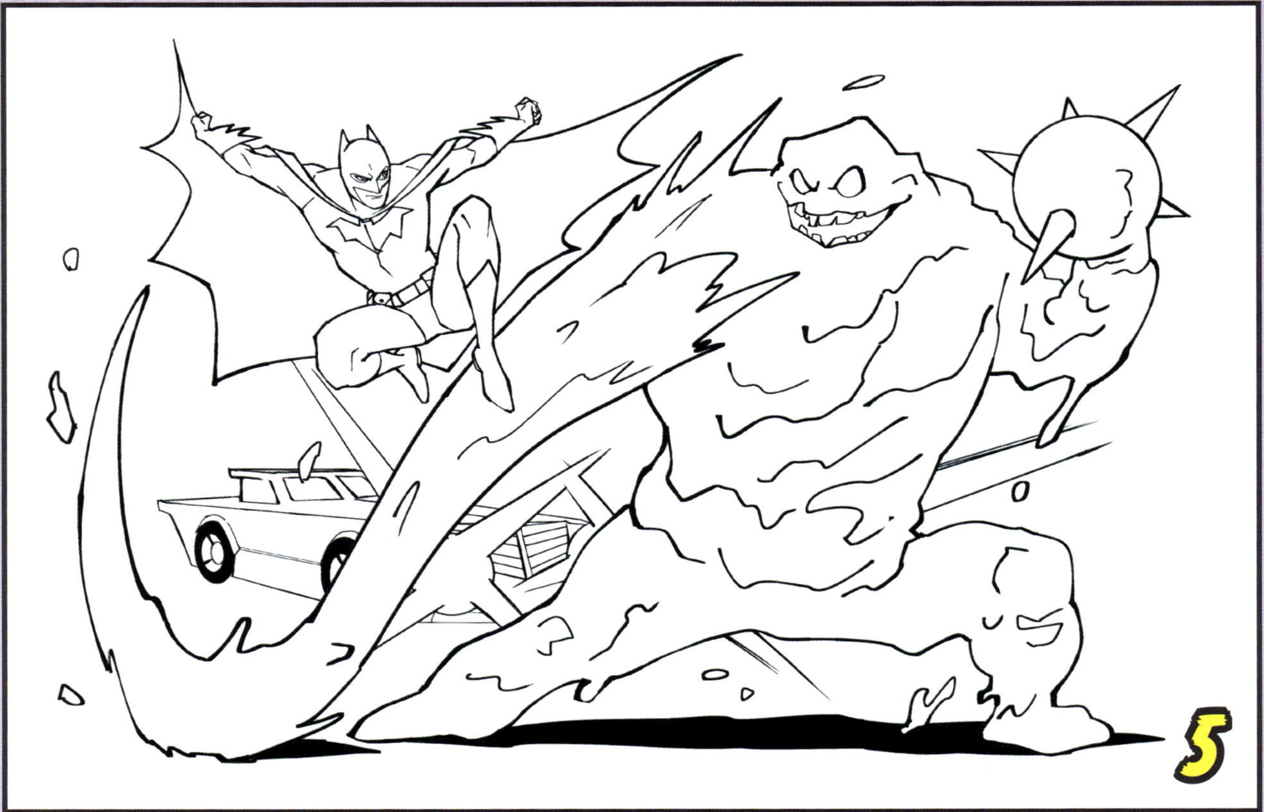
5

MORE MANGA DRAWING FUN!

Hart, Christopher. *Drawing Anime from Simple Shapes: Character Design Basics for All Ages.* New York: Drawing with Christopher Hart, 2020.

Whitten, Samantha. *Let's Draw Manga Chibi Characters.* Beverly, MA: Walter Foster Jr., 2023.

Yazawa, Nao. *Drawing and Painting Anime & Manga Faces: Step-by-Step Techniques for Creating Authentic Characters and Expressions.* Beverly, MA: Quarry Books, 2021.

MORE DC SUPER HERO FUN!

DC
BATMAN
ORIGAMI
AMAZING FOLDING PROJECTS FEATURING THE DARK KNIGHT
BY JOHN MONTROLL

DC
DC SUPER HEROES
KNOCK-KNOCK JOKES
BY MICHAEL DAHL & DONALD LEMKE
HA! HA! HA!

DC SUPER HEROES
ROBIN
AN ORIGIN STORY
DAHL · BRIZUELA

DC SUPER HEROES
YOU CHOOSE
BATMAN
THE TERRIBLE TRIO
12 POSSIBLE ENDINGS
BY LAURIE S. SUTTON

DC
BATMAN & ROBIN
ADVENTURES
HARLEY QUINN'S
CRAZY CREEPER CAPER
SIMONSON · VECCHIO

DC SUPER HERO ADVENTURES
DC
BATGIRL
AND THE
QUEEN OF GREEN
SUTTON · CASTELLANI

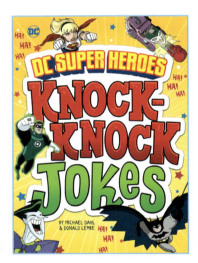

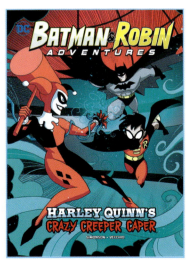